THE MERCHANT NAVY GOES TO WAR

Born of a long line of Welsh master mariners, it was inevitable that Bernard Edwards should follow the family tradition. He saw service as a cadet in merchant ships at the end of the Second World War. Later he became a master mariner and for fourteen years commanded general cargo ships trading mainly in the Middle and Far East. He left the sea in 1984 to begin a second career as an author and maritime journalist and now lives with his wife in a small village in rural Gwent far from the sound of the sea. Captain Edwards' research into the role of Britain's Merchant Navy during the war has left him with the deep conviction that the men whose skill and determination kept open the vital sea lanes of this country received little credit for the sacrifices they made. Previously published in hardback as *The Fighting Tramps*, this is not Bernard Edwards' only book on matters maritime. He is also the author of *They Sank the Red Dragon* and *The Grey Widow-Maker: Twenty-four Disasters at Sea.*

The Merchant Navy Goes to War

BERNARD EDWARDS

ROBERT HALE · LONDON

© *Bernard Edwards 1989*
First published in Great Britain 1989
Second (paperback) edition 1990

Robert Hale Limited
Clerkenwell House
Clerkenwell Green
London EC1R 0HT

British Library Cataloguing in Publication Data

Edwards, Bernard, *1926–*
    The fighting tramps: the Merchant Navy goes
    to war
    1. World War   2. Role of British merchant
    shipping
    I. Title
    940.54'5941

    ISBN 0–7090–4251–5

Photoset in Ehrhardt by
Derek Doyle and Associates, Mold, Clwyd.
Printed in Great Britain by
St Edmundsbury Press Limited, Bury St Edmunds, Suffolk.
Bound by WBC Bookbinders Limited.

Contents

For the men of the British tramps
who died in that unequal fight.

The world paid but a penny for its toll,
That which was priceless got the beggar's dole;
Men who fetcht beauty, iron, corn or oil
Scarce could keep beggar's bones about the
soul.

John Masefield, 'Pay'

Illustrations

PICTURE CREDITS

The author and publishers wish to thank the following sources for permission to reproduce the photographs used in this book. The Imperial War Museum, London: 1, 2, 5, 10, 11, 12, 13, 16; the Welsh Industrial & Maritime Museum, Cardiff: 3, 4, 6; A. Duncan, Gravesend: 7, 8, 9, 15; Reardon Smith Line, Cardiff: 14.

Acknowledgements

The author gratefully acknowledges the help given to him in the research for this book by the following sources and people:

Public Record Office, Kew; General Register and Record Office of Shipping and Seamen, Llandaff; Welsh Industrial and Maritime Museum, Cardiff; Imperial War Museum, London; Jim Evans, W.R. Henke, Dr David Jenkins, Captain W.S. Lewis, Haven Puxley, Captain C.L. Thomas, Captain Daniel Morley Williams.

Author's Note

This book is by way of a sequel to *They Sank the Red Dragon* (GPC Books, 1987), which dealt specifically with the role of the Welsh tramps in World War II. It has been written in much the same way, in that I have taken as a basis for each chapter the wartime reports lodged at the Public Record Office.

I have, as before, carried out considerable background research and drawn on my experience at sea to tell each story in my own words. In doing so, I am aware I have taken certain liberties and therefore left myself open to criticism and correction.

There are those who will argue that some of the ships featured were not really tramps. They may be right, for the dividing line between tramp and the cargo liner was at times very thin. I crave the forgiveness of those whom I may unintentionally have wronged.

Bernard Edwards   Llanvaches
                                                             1988

1 To War!

In the halcyon years leading up to World War II, Britain's merchant ships dominated the world's seaborne trade. British shipowners waxed fat, re-investing their profits in new tonnage, and their horizons became ever wider. It was claimed that, on any one day, an average of 2,500 ships flying the Red Ensign were at sea or at work in the various ports of the world. Such prestigious liner companies as P & O, Ellermans and Blue Funnel took the cream, but it was the old tramps of Runcimans, Ropners, Radcliffes and their many contemporaries that carried the greatest burden of the trade – and subsequently profited most.

Ironically, the men who sailed in these ships – the men who created the wealth – were those who benefited least. The general public saw them as a necessary evil; lower-class civilian sailors hawking their rust-bucket ships around the trade routes of the world to the greater glory of King and Empire. Shipowners exploited them, judges and titled ladies equated them with the scum of the earth. They drank, they fought and they fornicated, keeping solvent countless dockside pubs and whorehouses from Cardiff to Canton. Yet at their job they were the best the world has ever seen, resilient, resourceful, innovative and blessed with an unfailing sense of humour. Such were the men who crewed Britain's tramp ships of the 1930s.

The average British tramp of the day was of about 5,000 tons gross, blunt in the bow, rounded in the stern and capable of carrying a vast amount of bulk or general cargo. She boasted a forest of spindly derricks, her decks were cluttered with steam-belching winches, and her tall masts and funnel were reminiscent of a bygone age. Her propulsion unit, crammed into the smallest possible compartment to avoid wasting precious cargo space, was usually a basic but reliable triple-expansion, steam-reciprocating engine. Fed by three Scotch boilers, into the hungry furnaces of which her 'black gang' of scrawny firemen shovelled best Welsh steam coal, this ponderous machine produced a top speed of eight to nine knots – when the weather was kindly.

Accommodation for her crew was often no more than an afterthought, as though the shipowner was reluctant to burden his ship with structures that earned no freight – as indeed he was. The ratings lived in a dark, airless cavern under the forecastle head, sleeping in two-tiered bunks that rose and fell like high-speed lifts with every swell that passed under the bow. Her deck officers – the ruling hierarchy – bunked amidships, directly below the bridge, in cabins just big enough to swing the proverbial cat, of which there were always two or three on board to keep at bay the army of voracious rats which inhabited the cargo holds. Engineers spent their off-watch time in similar cabins perched on top of a steamy engine-room, beautifully warm in the British winter but uninhabitable in the tropics. Only captains and chief engineers enjoyed the luxury of their own bath and toilet; the rest took their place in a queue in the alleyway.

Navigational equipment was of the most rudimentary, conforming only to the minimum requirements laid down by the omnipotent Board of Trade, namely a magnetic compass, a deep-sea sounding lead and an alert lookout man. That is not to say that the standard of navigation was any the less for such limitations. Sextant and chronometer were put to good use, and it is much to the credit of their masters and deck officers that the tramps wandered to the far reaches of the earth and back with remarkably few casualties by stranding.

Unlike their more privileged sisters, the cargo liners, tramps had no regular or recognized itinerary. They were, for the most part, engaged in the cross trades, often leaving British shores laden down to their marks with Welsh coal and thereafter working the charter market between the diverse ports of the world, earning their keep as they went. It was not unusual for a ship to be away from her home port for up two years, shuttling coal from Barry to Rio de Janeiro, wheat from the River Plate to Shanghai, sugar from Surabaya to Bombay, and so on, ever circling the globe in search of employment.

Wages and conditions of service for the men sailing in the tramps were usually the minimum allowed under British law. A first mate holding a foreign-going master's certificate could expect to earn about £23 a month, an ordinary seaman £6. For these princely sums they were expected to work up to ten hours a day, seven days a week, and at any other time the safety of the ship or cargo required. There was no paid leave at the end of a voyage, no matter how long it lasted. If a man wished to spend time with his family, he had no alternative but to quit the ship and go off pay. While at sea, medical attention was confined to that which could be provided by the master of the vessel, whose expertise depended on his familiarity with the Ship Captain's Medical Guide, the Board of Trade's 'bible' on the treatment of the sick and injured. Yet treatment on board was often preferable to that offered by the half-trained quacks who masqueraded as company doctors in the far-flung outposts of the Empire. But afloat or ashore, baffling illnesses were frequently diagnosed as malingering, and woe betide the man who contracted 'lady sickness', as the seaman's shore-going occupational hazard was delicately described. VD was considered to be a self-inflicted disease, and the shipowner was not obliged to pay for the treatment of such.

The diet of the tramp-ship men – again dictated by the Board of Trade – would not have been acceptable in many Victorian workhouses. Salt beef, salt pork, potatoes half rotten after a few weeks in the locker, haricot beans, split peas, rice and oatmeal were the staple fare at sea, and in port were supplemented with – 'when procurable at a reasonable cost' – a limited amount of so-called fresh meat and fresh vegetables. Much of the food supplied by ship's chandlers, who regarded pigs and seamen as being roughly on a par, was of such poor quality that no self-respecting landsman would allow it near his plate. Nevertheless, even in the tramps, the time-honoured British sense of fair play prevailed and provisions, issued daily or weekly, were meticulously doled out by the pound and pint under the eagle eye of the ship's chief steward. It was their more fortunate brothers in the cargo liners, where a much higher standard of feeding was enjoyed, who coined the phrase 'pound & pint ships' to describe the Board of Trade victualling scale.

Without the benefit of air-conditioning, the tramp-ship men

sweated out their lifeblood in the tropics. Deaths from heat exhaustion, especially in the engine-room department, were commonplace. In the depths of winter they hovered on the fringe of hypothermia, their suffering only sometimes eased by a cranky, inefficient steam-heating system. In port, after working hours, both heating and electric lighting were often turned off in the interest of fuel economy, leaving them huddled around smoking oil lamps in overcoats and mufflers.

Little wonder that, in Britain alone, there were more than 150 charities dedicated to the care of merchant seamen.

What induced these men to sign on voyage after voyage, sure in the knowledge that they would endure such discomforts and indignities? Were they masochists, or just plain simple? Far from it. The 1930s had seen years of world economic depression, and the threat of unemployment was still a strong incentive, though by no means the main driving-force. The sea was in their blood, as it always has been in all successive generations of the island race. For the tramp-ship men, the sea held no image of romance – this they knew existed only in the fertile imagination of the fiction writer; but there was adventure to be had in plenty, and by this prospect they were all too easily seduced. They lived in a harsh, demanding environment, often akin to a prison afloat, but it was well-ordered society which looked after its own, and who knew what adrenalin-stirring challenge or sumptuous delight lay over the horizon? The awesome roar of the hurricane, the insidious, blinding fog that muffled the approach of danger – or perhaps the arms of a beautiful Japanese whore, whose gentle ministrations healed all wounds and stilled all longings. For the seamen, the horizon was always beckoning.

When war came in 1939, the tramp-ship men, like all British merchant seamen, took it in their stride. As civilians following an occupation demanding so much for such niggardly rewards, they might have been excused if they had been loath to face the additional dangers brought by war. Yet never once did they hesitate. No British merchant ship was ever held in port by its crew, even at the height of the Battle of the Atlantic, when to cross that ocean in a slow-moving merchant ship was to walk hand in hand with death for every minute of the day and night. Nor, when there was a need to supply arms to the Soviet Union via the Arctic route, did they flinch. German surface ships and aircraft, based in northern Norway, savaged them without mercy, while the ever-present U-boats continued to snap at their heels like the Hounds of Hell. Of those who died – and they were legion – the fortunate fell to the guns and torpedoes of the enemy, the luckless froze to death in minutes in the icy waters of the Arctic Sea. Those who were spared to reach their goals often endured round-the-clock bombing by German aircraft while in port. But the greatest indignity many of these men suffered was to be treated by their erstwhile Soviet allies as outcasts, tainted by the dread disease of capitalism.

Not that they fared any better at the hands of their own kind. Under British law, when a merchant ship was lost, even in wartime, the shipowner's obligation to pay wages to its crew went with it. There were some who took a more philanthropic view, but others closed the books the minute the ship disappeared beneath the waves. To die in the water unemployed was a distinction often awarded to the tramp-ship men. Those who survived a sinking found their ordeal was by no means over when they reached the shores of Britain: they were sent home in the clothes they stood up in, with a free railway warrant and half a crown in expenses to speed them on their way. It was almost as though their country was ashamed of them. And yet they still went back to sea, some staying ashore only long enough to get together some new kit.

Undoubtedly the greatest strains of the war at sea fell on the shoulders of the masters and deck officers of the tramp ships. Their charges were slow and maneouvred like the lumbering barges they were. Station-keeping in convoy was for these men an unending ordeal. On a dark, moonless night it required nerves of steel and the eyes of a cat; in poor visibility or stormy weather it was an impossibility. They straggled, they romped and they veered, becoming the easiest of targets for the stalking U-boats. The men in the engine-room suffered the tortures of the damned, never knowing when a torpedo might tear through the thin plates of the hull, sending their ship plunging to the bottom before they had chance to reach the first rung of the ladder to the deck. Burdened, as they so often were, with heavy bulk cargoes, the tramps sank like punctured tin cans filled with lead shot. For those who took to the lifeboats or rafts, the process of dying was more prolonged. Lacking protection from the sun and storms, and striving to exist on rations measured in ounces per day, many eventually succumbed to exposure, starvation, thirst or sheer mental exhaustion.

By the time the war finally ended, in August 1945, 29,180 British merchant seamen had lost their lives in the conflict, almost fifty per cent of them in the tramp ships. As I write, the tragic story of the loss of the cross-Channel ferry *Herald of Free Enterprise* fills television screens and newspapers from day to day. The British public are horrified and outraged that such a thing could happen to one of their ships. They have forgotten – or perhaps never knew – that in the years 1939-45 the awful drama of the *Herald of Free Enterprise* was being enacted in the deep oceans as often as fifteen times a week, every week, with the men of Britain's old tramps playing the lead roles. Within the pages of this book an attempt has been made to bring to life the stories of some of these men and their ships.

2   'A Game for Gentlemen'

The dark clouds of war were brushing the hilltops of Europe when, shortly after nightfall on 19 August 1939, seventeen sinister black shapes slipped out of Wilhelmshaven, motored in line ahead across Jade Bay and fanned out into the North Sea. The cream of Admiral Dönitz's undersea battle fleet was on its way to take up station off the western approaches to the British Isles. In its midst was *U-33*, commanded by Kapitän-Leutnant Hans-Wilhelm von Dresky, who, by his own admission, was a reluctant warrior.

It was not that von Dresky's courage or loyalty to his own country was in question, nor did he lack confidence in his crew or his boat. His men were hand-picked from the elite of the *Kriegsmarine*, and *U-33* was as formidible a weapon as any man could wish to command. Displacing 740 tons and 220 feet long, the new Type VII U-boat had a maximum range of 6,500 miles, with a top speed of 17 knots on the surface and 7.5 knots when submerged. She was armed with an 88 mm deck gun, one 37mm and two 20mm anti-aircraft guns and five 53 cm torpedo tubes. Von Dresky's problem was that he could just not see any reason for open conflict between two nations as closely linked as Britain and Germany.

To the U-boats, as they exchanged their last guarded signals before dispersing into the dark night, the threat of war was very real. Some 4,500 miles to the south-west, on the West Indian island of Cuba, a very different atmosphere prevailed. Here the sun was still high in a cloudless sky, the surf boomed good-naturedly on the white sands and the talk was of tobacco, sugar and the price of rum. In Puerto Padre, a small harbour on the north-east coast of the island, the British ship *Olivegrove* lay loading a full cargo of raw sugar, which she had been chartered to carry to Europe.

The 4,060-ton *Olivegrove*, built by Lithgows on the Clyde in 1929 and managed by David Alexander & Sons of Glasgow for the Grove Line, was very much the archetypal deep-sea tramp of her day. Her wide-bellied hull fell only a little short of the rectangular, her accommodation was equally unattractive and her triple-expansion, steam-reciprocating engine cranky and underpowered. But, despite her graceless lines, the *Olivegrove* was well cared for, her black hull and white superstructure showing only minimal signs of rust, and her teakwood bridge-house in a good state of repair and freshly varnished. She was grandly classed by her owners as a 'general trader', which in effect meant she was in the market to carry anything anywhere, providing the price was right and the water deep enough. Of her crew of thirty-three, the majority were Scots, as would be expected of a Glasgow ship, with a sprinkling of English, Irish, 'Tiger Bay Arabs'(the nickname of Somali seamen living in the Butetown area of Cardiff) and the inevitable fifteen-year-old galley boy from Barry, South Wales, from which port she had sailed in ballast in late July that year.

On the lower bridge of the *Olivegrove*, her master, forty-six-year-old Captain James Barnetson of Leith, paced the scrubbed wooden deck deep in thought, stopping from time to time to run a critical eye over the slings of bagged sugar as they came swinging over the ship's rail. His mind was occupied with two weighty problems, both complex and both disturbing.

Uppermost in his thoughts was the weather, for early autumn in the West Indies is a time of danger, when hurricanes, spawned in the open Atlantic to the east of Barbados, sweep north-westerly, bringing with them devastating winds, mountainous seas and torrential rain. Cuba stands square in their path, and to be caught in harbour during such a storm could spell disaster for the *Olivegrove*. Had the time been thirty years on, Barnetson would have been able to call on a highly sophisticated weather-forcasting organization backed by satellites, but in 1939 he had only the barometer and his own experience to warn of approaching danger. He was unlikely to rest easy until his ship was loaded and heading for the open sea.

And then there were the storm clouds of another kind

gathering on the other side of the world. Since Neville Chamberlain had returned from Munich in September 1938 waving his worthless piece of paper and promising 'peace in our time', the momentum of German expansionism had been speeding up. Czechoslovakia had gone the way of Austria, and it seemed Poland was about to follow suit, flattened under the marching jackboots of Hitler's legions. For the second time in a generation the talk was of war between Britain and Germany, and this troubled James Barnetson. In the Great War of 1914-18, such had been the horrors of trench warfare on the Western Front that the sacrifices made by Britain's merchant seamen had gone almost unnoticed, in spite of the loss of 2,479 ships and 14,789 seamen. Barnetson had been a young man in that war and had good cause to remember the hideous toll it had exacted among his shipmates. It was his fervent hope that such a thing would never happen again, but he knew in his heart that it was now as inevitable as the coming of the next dawn.

The *Olivegrove* sailed from Puerto Padre on the afternoon of 22 August and, loaded down to her tropical marks, wallowed like a pregnant duck as soon as she left the shelter of the land. It was obvious to Barnetson that his ship would not break any records on the run to the north, but he was well used to this state of affairs. His immediate and most pressing object was to clear the mass of cays and islands that make up the archipelago of the Bahamas, for here, caught by a hurricane, the *Olivegrove* would have no room to maneouvre.

As it turned out, Barnetson's fears proved groundless. The weather remained fine and calm and, thirty-six hours after leaving Puerto Padre, the *Olivegrove* was clear of the Bahamas and settled down on her long, diagonal run across the Atlantic. In accordance with common practice in the charter market, where cargoes often change hands overnight, the port of discharge for the *Olivegrove*'s cargo had not yet been declared. She was heading for 'Land's End for orders', meaning Barnetson would be notified by radio of his destination a few days before reaching British waters. By past experience, those on board knew this would almost certainly be London, Liverpool or Glasgow, with the ship's Scottish home port being a hot favourite. Whatever decision was taken by the wheelers and dealers of the Baltic Exchange, ahead of the *Olivegrove* lay a voyage of 3,700 miles, sixteen or seventeen days during which a great deal might happen.

Oblivious to the stratagems of man, the *Olivegrove* pushed north-eastwards under an untroubled sky, dipping her blunt bows into a boisterous sea with gay abandon. It was as though she sensed she was on her way home. The miles seemed to fly by, and before long the homeward-bound spirit was rampant throughout the ship. Paintbrushes worked overtime, stores and repair lists were drawn up and shore-going clothes brought out of musty wardrobes to air on deck.

Meanwhile, half a world away, Germany signed a non-aggression pact with the Soviet Union and the end of two decades of uneasy peace in Europe drew near.

On Friday 1 September German tanks rolled across the Polish frontier, and the die was cast. Two days later, at 11 a.m. on the 3rd, when the *Olivegrove* was 350 miles north-west of Flores in the Azores, where Sir Richard Grenville had fought his last battle, Prime Minister Neville Chamberlain announced that Britain was at war with Germany. Within five minutes, the following radio signal went out from Wilhelmshaven to the U-boat fleet:

1105/3/9/39 FROM NAVAL HIGH COMMAND STOP TO COMMANDERS-IN-CHIEF AND COM-MANDERS AFLOAT STOP GREAT BRITAIN AND FRANCE HAVE DECLARED WAR ON GERMANY STOP BATTLE STATIONS IMMEDIATE IN ACCORDANCE WITH BATTLE INSTRUCTIONS FOR THE NAVY ALREADY PROMULGATED.

At this time, *U-33* was patrolling to the west of Ireland, and it was with a decided lack of enthusiasm that Hans-Wilhelm von Dresky opened his small safe and took out the sealed orders he had carried with him from Wilhelmshaven. He was instructed to move south to cover the south-western approaches to the English Channel and there attack and sink any British ships sighted.

The news of the outbreak of war was received philosophically on board the *Olivegrove*. The general consensus of opinion was that they would have little to fear from the Germans; the omnipotent Royal Navy would look after them. But there were those who said otherwise, and they spoke with the voice of authority and experience. Barnetson himself, his chief officer William Wilson and Chief Engineer Duncan Robb had lived through the other war and had no leanings toward complacency. The *Olivegrove* was immediately brought onto a war footing, with watches doubled, extra look-outs posted and the ship darkened at night. That evening her radio officer reported plaintive cries for help from the passenger ship *Athenia*, torpedoed without warning some 250 miles north-west of Ireland. For Britain's merchant fleet, the killing war had begun.

Noon sights on 7 September put the *Olivegrove* 420 miles to the west-south-west of Land's End. The weather remained fine, visibility was good and she was making a respectable 9½ knots. When Barnetson left Second Officer John Alexander in charge of the bridge and went below for his mid-day meal, he was well pleased. Within twenty-four hours, his ship would come under the protection of the Royal Navy's patrols, and the worst danger would be past.

Barnetson returned to the bridge less than an hour later, his appetite curbed. After a word with Alexander, he moved out into the port wing and began to pace up and down briskly, mindful of the extra portion of duff he had indulged in. He was on his fifth lap of the fifteen-foot-long deck when a movement on the horizon caused him to halt in mid-stride. He raised his binoculars and, as the long, grey shape with its fin-like conning-tower came into focus, let out a bitter curse, not so much at the sight of the enemy submarine (he had no doubt that this *was* the enemy) but at the gross unfairness of his lot. He had brought his ship and her cargo over 3,500 miles without incident and was almost in reach of sanctuary, and now it seemed his efforts would come to naught. The *Olivegrove* was unarmed and therefore at the mercy of the approaching U-boat.

Frustration suddenly turned to anger, and Barnetson stormed into the wheel-house, ordered the helm hard to starboard and gave a savage double ring on the engine-room telegraph, calling for emergency full speed. Damn the Germans! He would make a run for it.

In the conning-tower of *U-33*, Hans-Wilhelm von Dresky also felt a surge of anger as he saw the merchantman contemptuously offer him her squat stern. Having no wish to add to the furore caused by the sinking without warning of the *Athenia*, he had been making his approach to the British ship strictly in accordance with the Prize Regulations laid down by the Hague Convention. *U-33* was on the surface, flying code flags ordering the merchant ship to heave to, and her signal lamp was flashing the same message. How typical of the British to complicate things!

On the *Olivegrove*'s bridge, which was shaking violently as Chief Engineer Robb worked his engine up to maximum possible revolutions, Barnetson braced his shoulder against a stanchion and examined the U-boat through his binoculars. She was about five miles off on the starboard quarter and trimmed down so that she was almost awash. The flags she flew were too small to read at that distance; nor could Barnetson read the flashing lamp. The German signaller, who, like all naval men, clearly regarded merchant seamen as blind half-wits, was sending his message so slowly that it was impossible to string the dots and dashes together to make words. But, even so, the meaning of the signals was unmistakeable.

The U-boat's deck gun now caught Barnetson's attention: it was manned and trained on the *Olivegrove* with obvious intent. As he watched, there was a flash from the muzzle of the gun, and a shell whined over his head. This, he knew, was the final warning to heave to. He chewed his lip and considered the situation. The U-boat was making a good six knots more than the *Olivegrove*, so he had no real hope of running away. Given a gun, however small, he would have been tempted to make a fight of it. He had fought the sea all his life and never given a thought to surrender, whatever the odds against him, but this time he was impotent, having no weapon to pit against this enemy other than his seamanship. He could continue to run, keeping the *Olivegrove*'s stern to the U-boat but sooner or later would come the hail of well-aimed shells or the silent torpedo. The end result could only be grieving widows and fatherless children in Glasgow, Liverpool and Cardiff.

With a hopeless shrug, Barnetson walked back into the wheel-house and rang the engine-room telegraph to stop. By this time, Second Officer Alexander had succeeded in deciphering the U-boat's signals. As expected, the order was to stop and abandon ship. Nodding agreement, Barnetson told

Alexander to pass the word for boat stations.

There was no panic in abandoning ship. With as little enthusiasm as they normally showed at a routine lifeboat drill, the *Olivegrove*'s crew swung out their two boats and lowered them to the water before boarding. It seemed like a bad dream from which they would soon awake. Equally unhurried, Barnetson retrieved the ship's confidential books from the safe in his cabin, placed them in the weighted bag provided and hurled them into the sea. He then gathered up the few papers he would need to conclude the voyage and went to his boat.

The two loaded lifeboats pulled away from the *Olivegrove*'s side, leaving her stopped and rolling gently in the swell. Once she had been a bustling ship with a purpose; now she looked strangely pathetic: a ship with a past but no future. The U-boat was four to five miles off her starboard beam, waiting like a hooded executioner.

As soon as the lifeboats were clear, the U-boat moved in at full speed, submerging when she was within a mile of the ship. From the stern of his boat, Barnetson watched and waited with a lump in his throat that threatened to choke him. He heard the dull thump and saw the *Olivegrove* shudder and then throw up a great cloud of water, smoke and steam. Hit squarely amidships, she took only six minutes to die. There were tears in Barnetson's eyes as she slipped beneath the waves.

Meanwhile the U-boat had re-surfaced and was moving back towards the drifting lifeboats. Barnetson had seen photographs of German submarines in illustrated magazines, and he estimated this to be one of the largest class. As the long, predatory shape drew near, he made mental notes of her appearance. Her grey-green paintwork looked new, and she mounted a short-barrelled, three-inch or 3½ inch gun just forward of her conning-tower.

The submarine stopped within fifty yards of the lifeboats, and a voice called for the captain to come alongside. Barnetson, suspicious, yet curious to meet the man who had sunk his ship, hailed back and ordered his men to pull for the U-boat.

As the lifeboat bumped alongside, Barnetson noted that the U-boat's hull was free of barnacles, but she had three-inch-long grass growing just below the waterline. In differing circumstances, he might have been amused at his automatic critical assessment of the hull of another man's ship, but he clambered aboard the U-boat unsmiling, clutching the few papers that were all that remained of his own command.

Hans-Wilhelm von Dresky did not volunteer his own name but shook Barnetson by the hand and in heavily accented English requested to see his papers. While the German commander studied the documents, Barnetson studied him. He was tall and very thin, with sharp features and dark hair, and he appeared to be between thirty-five and forty years old. His chin carried a good two weeks of growth but he showed no signs of fatigue.

The German returned the papers, saying, 'I am sorry I have to sink your ship, Captain. But why does your Mr Chamberlain want to make war on us? We do not want war.'

Somewhat taken aback by the man's reasonableness, Barnetson shrugged and answered that he, personally, had no wish to make war on anyone.

They were now joined in the conning-tower by two other officers. Both were unshaven, in their mid or early thirties, and spoke good English. They were extremely polite and friendly. One, whom Barnetson took to be the engineer, was a golf fanatic and, having learned that Barnetson hailed from Leith, enthused about St Andrews and the holidays he had spent there. The conversation, which was all of a general nature, went on for nearly two hours. The Germans showed no animosity towards Barnetson and asked no compromising questions. They gave the British captain the distinct impression that they, and the commander in particular, were whole-heartedly opposed to the war with Britain.

As they stood shoulder to shoulder in the conning-tower, chatting genially like old friends in a pub, Barnetson began to feel a certain sympathy for these men. Like himself, they were seamen caught up in a war that was not of their making. He reached the point where the situation had become so unreal that he felt the need to pinch himself, when a younger officer joined them and gave the Nazi salute, inviting Barnetson to '*Heil Hitler!*' It then came home to him forcibly that these men had just sunk his ship and probably would have killed him and his crew if necessary. When the U-boat commander shook his hand again and said he was free to go, Barnetson wasted no time in returning to the lifeboat.

Back with his crew, Barnetson conferred with Chief Officer Wilson, and it was agreed that the two boats should make for the island of Fastnet, off the southern coast of Ireland. The distance to go was some 290 miles, and if the weather did not deteriorate, it was estimated they would make a landfall in about three days. A daunting prospect for open boats, perhaps, but they had no other option. Hoisting sail, they set off to the north-east.

Unbeknown to the *Olivegrove*'s survivors, they did have another option. Von Dresky was about to make recompense for the sinking of their ship. He had contacted the American passenger liner *Washington*, and for the next nine hours *U-33* circled the lifeboats at a discreet distance. When the *Washington* hove in sight at about 9.30 that night, von Dresky fired two Very lights before making off to the west. As he watched the U-boat motor away, Barnetson was forced to conclude that he had received his first taste of this war at the hands of a gentleman. Would it always be that way in the coming years, he wondered.

All thirty-three men of the *Olivegrove* were picked up by the *Washington* that night and landed safely in Cork twenty-four hours later.

The *Olivegrove* had been Hans-Wilhelm von Dresky's first victim. His subsequent war record was neither long nor impressive. *U-33* sank only ten more ships, six being mere fishing-boats, before she was caught and sunk in the Firth of Clyde by HMS *Gleaner* on 12 February 1940. The owners of the *Olivegrove* fared little better, losing their entire fleet of eleven vessels to the U-boats during the war.

3   Ropner's Gunboats

On a sunless morning in October 1939, Swansea's King's Dock was not a sight to inspire men to poetry. Even the most sombre of Welsh bards would have been hard pressed to sing its praises. A leaden sky, hovering at mast-top height, deposited a steady curtain of drizzle into an atmosphere already dark with suspended coal dust. From the direction of the Bristol Channel, a south-westerly wind keened in over the breakwaters, sending black-topped wavelets scudding across the dock, pushing before them fragments of rotting driftwood, clusters of empty beer bottles and an obscene fleet of discarded condoms.

Moored bow to stern under the towering coal-hoists, two of Sir Robert Ropner's best bared their hatches to the rumbling, cascading coal. On the quayside, clustered around the gangways of both ships, drums of paint, coils of rope, cases and cartons were piled in untidy heaps, indicating that the voyage stores had arrived – as always, when the ships were at their busiest and dirtiest.

The *Heronspool* and *Stonepool*, if not sister ships – for they were out of different yards, were certainly first cousins, and typical British Tramps. Their box-like hulls, sparse superstructure and tall, 'Woodbine' funnels stamped them as products of the bustling shipyards of the north-west coast of England, designed to carry maximum cargo at minimum cost, with the end result of maximum profit for their owners. The *Stonepool* was the younger of the two by a year, having left her slipway in 1928. Both were registered at West Hartlepool and owned by the Pool Shipping Company, a subsidiary of Sir Robert Ropner & Co Ltd of Darlington.

The two ships were near to their marks and within hours of sailing. Commanded by Captain Sydney Batson, the 5,202-ton

Heronspool was about to set off for Montreal with a full cargo of anthracite. The *Stonepool*, slightly smaller at 4,803 tons gross, commanded by Captain Albert White, had on board steam coal for the bunker station at the Cape Verde islands.

Batson and White, friends of long standing and one-time shipmates, had enjoyed the pleasure of each other's company while their ships occupied adjacent berths in Swansea, but now they were anxious to be on their way. October, as they well knew, is when autumn turns to winter in the North Atlantic, the time when that tempestuous ocean begins to unsheath its claws in earnest. Of the two ships, the *Heronspool* faced the most arduous voyage by far. Her route to the Gulf of St Lawrence would take her far to the north, across 2,400 miles of inhospitable ocean, where the additional danger of icebergs lurked. For her crew there would be no escape from the full rigours of the on-coming winter. The *Stonepool*, on the other hand, was southbound, and every turn of her screw would bring her nearer to the more gentle ways of the tropics. A month or so earlier, either voyage would have been routine for the tramps, but now there were the hazards of war to face. Despite the Navy's claim that the Germans had already lost half their ocean-going U-boats, thirty-three British merchant ships, totalling 164,205 tons, had so far been sunk – a ship for every day of the war.

As a sure sign that the noose around Britain's sea lanes was expected to tighten even further, during their stay in the Bristol Channel the Ropner ships had each been equipped with a World War I vintage four-inch gun mounted on the stern and a light machine-gun for use against aircraft. In charge of the manning and maintenance of this armament were two experienced gunlayers of the newly formed Defensively Equipped Merchant Ships (DEMS) force. Able Seamen Gunners John Hayter and John Pearson, both Royal Navy pensioners recalled to active service for the duration, while enjoying the relaxed atmosphere in the merchant ships, were already experiencing misgivings about their new roles. Pearson, sailing in the *Heronspool*, and Hayter, in the *Stonepool*, had been handed the unenviable task of forming guns' crews from among the merchant seamen. It was quite obvious to both that a great deal of training and motivation would be needed before these unruly civilian sailors would be in a fit state to swap shells with the enemy. The Navy men had yet to be exposed to the astonishing adaptability of the 'Pound & Pint Sailors'.

The problems of the two gunlayers were insignificant compared with those faced by Captains Batson and White. They had been informed, somewhat peremptorily, by the Admiralty that their ships were to sail in convoy from Milford Haven to a point 400 miles out into the Atlantic before proceeding independently. Like all men who commanded merchant ships, Batson and White disliked and distrusted the convoy system. They felt it unfairly restricted their freedom of movement and imposed an unnecessary extra burden on themselves and their officers. In the interest of good station-keeping, watches would have to be doubled on the bridge and in the engine-room, which, in ships already operating on the absolute minimum of men, meant increased hours on duty and precious little sleep for those concerned. It also seemed to them ludicrous to bunch a lot of slow-moving merchantmen together, so that a U-boat, having found one, would find all. Was it not far better to allow the ships to go their own separate ways and let the U-boats do the hunting? In their considered opinion, the open sea was a good place to get lost in.

On Friday 6 October the *Heronspool* and *Stonepool*, down to their Winter North Atlantic marks, left Swansea within hours of each other. On the short, eight-hour passage around the Welsh coast, hoses and brushes were broken out and the crews of both vessels tackled the thick layer of coal dust that covered every exposed inch of deck and superstructure. By the time they sailed into Milford Haven, one of the largest deep-water harbours in the world, the tramps were passably clean but their crews exhausted.

Fortuitously, the convoy was not yet fully assembled, and three days were passed at anchor in the shelter of the Haven, during which Batson and White used every daylight hour in fully preparing their ships for the voyage to come. The last of the ubiquitous coal dust was chased away, hastily loaded stores were consigned to their correct lockers, and the securing of derricks and hatch-covers was double checked. It would not do to venture into the Western Ocean unprepared.

At 07.00 on 10 October, the two Ropner ships hove up

anchor and, in company with seven others and escorted by a single destroyer, sailed from Milford Haven. It was a fresh autumn morning, with the whitecaps tumbling and the enticing smell of frying bacon in the air. As the ships rounded St Ann's Head and, one by one, pointed their bows to the west, more than a few hearts beat faster in anticipation of the unknown. The proposed arrangement was to join forces off the Smalls with seven other ships, which had left Liverpool on the previous evening. Unfortunately, the most carefully laid plans often come to grief, and this one was no exception. Three hours after, the Bristol Channel ships were off the Smalls lighthouse, which guards the south-west corner of Wales, but there was no sign of the Liverpool ships. To wait off the Smalls, in full view of prowling U-boats and aircraft, was out of the question. There was no alternative but to carry on out to sea.

At daybreak on the 11th the convoy was eighty miles to the west of the Smalls when a circling Sunderland and columns of smoke on the horizon astern announced the belated arrival of the Liverpool ships. Due to the slow speed of one of their number, the Cardiff ship *Leeds City*, which was flying light, they had been over four hours late at the rendezvous.

Under the direction of the Convoy Commodore, who flew his flag in the *Bolton Hall*, another West Hartlepool tramp, the fourteen ships formed up in columns and set off to the west, zigzagging at 8½ knots. Escorting them, the destroyers *Imogen* and *Ilex*, their bow waves creaming, made broad sweeps ahead and astern, with look-outs combing the horizon and asdics constantly probing the depths for signs of the enemy. Overhead, the great four-engined Sunderland circled slowly, its guns and depth-charges ready to ward off attack from above or below. Convoy OB 17 was operational and in good hands.

In spite of the fact that this was the first convoy of the war for the merchant ships, station-keeping was good. But before many miles had been covered, it became evident that the designated convoy speed was beyond the reach of some of its ageing participants. Within an hour, half had become stragglers, among them the *Heronspool* and *Stonepool*. At 09.30 the commodore reduced speed to eight knots and ordered the stragglers to steam on steady courses in order to catch up with the main body of the convoy. A moderate swell was running in from the west and, although the two Ropner ships struggled valiantly, they dropped further and further astern. Sydney Batson and Arthur White began to regret the mistaken pride in their ships which had prompted them to declare top speeds of nine knots when joining the convoy.

At 06.45 on the 12th, when full daylight revealed the horizon, the *Heronspool* and *Stonepool* found they were alone on an empty sea. They were then 120 miles to the south-west of Fastnet and some hundred miles from the agreed dispersal point of the convoy. Realizing the futility of continuing the charade of keeping station on a non-existent convoy, Batson and White decided to part company and go their separate ways. After a brief exchange of goodbyes by signal lamp, the *Heronspool* continued to the west at a more leisurely pace, while the *Stonepool* sheered off to the south.

Night was closing in when Batson joined his chief officer, Charles Clifford, on the bridge of the *Heronspool*. The weather remained fair, but Batson was becoming concerned at the rising swell. To his experienced eye this indicated a heavy blow far out in the Atlantic. He was, in fact, correct, for 800 miles to the west the American liner *Manhattan* was reporting 'tremendous seas', as a result of which thirty of her passengers were injured.

For a while the two men stood in the open wing of the bridge, discussing ship's business and the voyage ahead. To them, it still seemed unlikely that the war would upset their routine to a great extent. In ten days, weather permitting, they would be in the Gulf of St Lawrence and beginning the 900-mile passage up river to Montreal. Once there, and far removed from the shooting war, they would spend a pleasant, if busy, week or so discharging the anthracite, then, if they were lucky, load a full cargo of timber or wood pulp, returning home in time for Christmas. It was all very hypothetical and unlikely, but then seamen are incurable optimists.

The tranquil scene changed rapidly. As the stand-by man on the bridge struck four bells, indicating the end of the first dog watch, the look-out on the forecastle head reported a ship on the port bow. Batson and Clifford, instantly alert, raised and focused their binoculars.

On the the darkening horizon they sighted a large tanker at about five miles off and apparently stopped. Batson was about to order his chief officer to contact the tanker by lamp when he became aware of the long, low outline of a submarine on the surface close to the other ship. The first flash of gunfire was enough to confirm that he had stumbled on the enemy in the act of savaging his prey.

For a brief moment, steeped in the ancient code of the sea that dictates no seaman shall turn his back on another in distress, Batson was tempted to intervene, to open fire on the U-boat with his newly acquired four-inch. But he was quick to realize the futility of such action. Although he had an experienced man in his gunlayer, Able Seaman John Pearson, the *Heronspool*'s scratch gun's crew were complete newcomers to the art of naval gunnery. They had, in fact, yet to fire the four-inch. Batson shook his head and ordered the helm hard to starboard. He must think of his own ship and run away before she too became a victim of the U-boat.

Batson's next, and instinctive, move was to order Chief Officer Clifford to sound the pre-arranged signal for action stations. This was a series of twelve short blasts on the steam whistle. Its sounding was to have dire consequences for the *Heronspool* and her crew.

Five miles away, in the conning-tower of *U-48*, Kapitän-Leutnant Herbert Schultze peered into the gathering dusk and grunted with satisfaction as another 88 mm shell slammed into the helpless tanker. His victim was, as he would learn later, the 14,115-ton Frenchman *Emile Miguet*, which had sailed from Jamaica before the outbreak of war and was unarmed. Her crew had already taken to the boats, and she was burning fiercely. Soon she would slip beneath the waves in a cloud of steam and smoke to double the tonnage *U-48* had sent to the bottom in these first few weeks of the war. Herbert Schultze was well on his way to becoming Germany's top-scoring U-boat ace.

The faint sound of the *Heronspool*'s steam whistle echoing across the water brought Schultze spinning around. He raised his binoculars, and a grim smile played around his lips as, on the blur of the horizon astern, he caught sight of the squat stern of the tramp as she made off to the north-west. Schultze had good cause to smile, for *U-48*, a Type VII boat, was capable of sixteen knots on the surface. There was ample time to finish off the tanker before going after the latest victim to walk uninvited into his net.

Meanwhile, aboard the *Heronspool*, unaware that he had

unwittingly announced his presence to the enemy, Batson was making every effort to save his ship. Gunlayer Pearson and his crew of eager amateurs were at their battle stations around the stern gun, while Chief Engineer Charles Dobson was below, coaxing every possible revolution out of the *Heronspool*'s hissing, thumping engine. Darkness was now almost complete and, as there would be no moon, escape into the night seemed a good possibility.

An hour passed, then two, and Batson dared to entertain hopes that his plan had succeeded. The night was as black as a pit, the sky clear and star-studded, so that the *Heronspool* seemed to be steaming along in a dark, empty void. Only the phosphorescence rolling away from her blunt bows revealed her presence, as she zigzagged hurriedly to the north-east.

At 20.00 they went through the routine of changing watches, but although men moved aside to make way for their reliefs, there was no standing down. On the bridge, Batson and Clifford stood side by side, staring silently astern, their faces showing the strain as they willed away the miles. They had no doubts that the U-boat was by now in pursuit.

U-48 was a lot closer than they had anticipated. The sound of eight bells was still ringing in the air when there was the loud crack of a gun and a column of water shot skywards close on the *Heronspool*'s starboard quarter. Kapitän-Leutnant Schultze had arrived to claim his fifth victim of the war.

Uncertain of his attacker's position, Batson could only press on at all speed, praying that the torpedo he feared would not come. Then, twenty minutes later, it was Schultze's turn to give himself away. Unsure of the *Heronspool*'s identity and perhaps unwilling this early in the war to make the mistake of sinking an innocent neutral, he ordered his signalman to challenge the unknown ship by lamp.

Batson saw the interrogating flash of the lamp and shortly afterwards was able to distinguish the dark outline of a submarine on his port quarter. He now had only two choices. He could stop and take to the boats, or run and fight. No one could have blamed him if he had taken the easy way out, for the submarine had twice the speed of his ship and, unlike the *Heronspool*'s, her gun's crew would be trained to a peak of perfection. Yet it took the merchant captain only a few seconds to make up his mind. Crossing to the engine-room telegraph, he gave a double ring for emergency full speed and then passed the order for the stern gun to open fire.

Crouching by the four-inch on the poop, where they had been at action stations for more than two hours, Gunlayer Pearson and his crew needed no urging on. Within seconds of their receiving the order to open fire, the first shell was in the breech and the U-boat in their sights. The ancient gun thundered and recoiled. Working swiftly, with only the occasional fumble, the crew cleared the breech, swabbed out, loaded and fired again. No fall of shot was observed, but the U-boat was seen to dive in a hurry. The first round was to the *Heronspool*.

On the bridge, Batson gave the order to cease fire and made another bid to escape. Hauling around to the west, he steamed at full speed, once again hoping to take cover in the darkness. In the engine-room, Charles Dobson, who had been torpedoed in the 1914-18 war, needed no urging to push his already hard-pressed engine to its utmost limits.

Two more wearying hours passed with no further sign of the U-boat, and Batson, now fearing an underwater attack, resumed zigzagging. He cursed roundly when, half an hour later, the submarine was seen by the light of the stars creeping up astern on the surface. The *Heronspool*'s four-inch opened fire, and two shots were seen to fall close to the U-boat, which immediately dived again.

And so the running battle went on, with *U-48* surfacing from time to time to swap shells with the stubborn little tramp that refused to surrender. Gunlayer Pearson, who had earlier entertained great doubts about the ability of his ragbag of a gun's crew, began visibly to glow with pride. These men – his men – were good. They fought with a careless precision that was perhaps born of countless battles in dockside pubs around the world. They had then, as they did now, stood shoulder to shoulder, sailors, firemen and stewards, defending the good name of the *Heronspool*. Even the youngest member of the crew, fourteen-year-old deckboy Frank Elders, demonstrated his contempt for the enemy by appearing on the gun platform with mugs of tea during each lull in the firing.

But the fight was between a crack German war-machine and a civilian ship pushed to her utmost limits and armed with an ancient gun crewed by amateurs. There could be only one end. Shortly after midnight, *U-48* landed a shell close on the *Heronspool*'s starboard side which sent her rolling on her beam ends. When she righted herself, Batson glanced at the wheel-house clock. Friday the 13th had arrived.

The end came an hour later, when, at 01.00, the U-boat dived and minutes later the *Heronspool* was rocked by a violent explosion which lifted her out of the water. Debris showered down on the bridge, and the ship took a heavy list to port. The torpedo had caught her in her forward hatch. Angry and at the same time sad, Batson reached for the whistle lanyard to sound the signal for boat stations. His old ship had fought her last fight.

At the first urgent tug of the lanyard, the whistle jammed wide open, and its mournful shriek added to the confusion reigning in the stricken ship. On the poop, Pearson and his crew struggled to extricate themselves from the wreckage of the gun platform, which had collapsed under them when the torpedo struck. In the wireless-room, Radio Officer George Haresnape, resisting the temptation to run, bent over his key and began tapping out a plaintive call for help.

In spite of the increasing list, the blackness of the night and the unnerving shriek of the whistle, there was no visible panic. Having supervised the dumping overboard of the secret code and signal books, Batson went to the boat-deck, where Chief Officer Clifford was already preparing the two lifeboats for lowering. As the ship was now well down by the head, Batson wasted no time in ordering his crew into the boats. Assisted by the stalwart Gunlayer Pearson and Able Seaman Brown, one of the gun's crew, he then lowered both boats to the water. Once the lifeboats were clear of the ship, the three men followed by jumping overboard.

Fortunately the sea was calm, and the boats were able to lie to close to the sinking ship, waiting for the dawn and the help they hoped would come. The *Heronspool*, tough, Tyne-built ship that she was, took a long time to die. She was still afloat when, shortly before dawn next day, the American passenger liner *President Harding* arrived, having raced through the night to answer George Haresnape's call for help.

The cold waters of the Atlantic finally closed over the

Heronspool as her lifeboats reached the side of the brilliantly lit *President Harding*. The old tramp had hung on until her men were in safe hands.

As Sydney Batson and his men clambered up the side of the American liner, ninety miles to the south-west, the *Stonepool* was peacefully following her normal early morning routine. Captain Albert White, sipping at a mug of hot, strong tea, was on the bridge waiting to see the sun over the horizon. In the wing, the *Stonepool*'s chief officer, Peter Love, busied himself with morning star-sights. Neither man was aware of the fate of the *Heronspool*.

The weather was holding good, and the *Stonepool* was forging her way southwards at a steady, if not impressive, eight knots and rolling easily in the long Atlantic swell. Yet Albert White was uneasy. He was not normally a superstitious man, but it was Friday the 13th and the ship was still in an area known to be the haunt of marauding U-boats.

They grey dawn turned to a promising sunrise. Peter Love completed working out his star-sights and plotted the ship's position on the chart. The *Stonepool* was 430 miles to the west of Ushant, with 1,942 miles to go to her destination, St Vincent in the Cape Verde Islands.

Looking up from the position chit handed to him by Chief Officer Love, White let his gaze wander around the deserted horizon. So far, so good. he walked out into the port wing of the bridge and leaned on the well-scrubbed taffrail, deep in thought. With an average day's run of only 190 miles, it was a long haul to St Vincent, but there would be compensations. In two more days, at the most, they would be in warmer weather and far enough away from the Western Approaches to be safe from attack by U-boats. There was always the possibility of a German surface raider being at large, but then, the ocean was a big place ...

White broke off from his reverie and reached for his binoculars. The early morning haze was lifting and he had spotted what appeared to be the funnel of a ship, hull down on the horizon to port. A homeward-bounder heading for the Bristol Channel, White decided, not without a pang of envy.

The distorting veil of mist suddenly lifted, and the funnel

became the conning-tower of a submarine on the surface, less than three miles off the *Stonepool*. White dived for the whistle lanyard just as the submarine's gun barked. *U-42*, commanded by Kapitän-Leutnant Rolf Dau, as yet unblooded in this war, had found her first likely victim.

The U-boat's first shell fell well ahead of the *Stonepool*, Dau's gunners having over-estimated the slow-moving merchantmen's speed. Without hesitation, White swung his ship hard to starboard, presenting her stern to the attacker. Like his old shipmate, Sydney Batson, Albert White had decided to fight and run.

Gunlayer John Hayter and his crew, which included Third Officer Leonard Corney and Chief Steward John Shipman, had reached their gun before the whistle finished sounding action stations. By the time the *Stonepool*'s stern had swung through 90 degrees and the U-boat came into their sights, the four-inch was loaded and ready. Within two minutes of *U-42*'s first shell landing, the *Stonepool* fired back.

Over the next ten minutes a fierce gun battle raged. White, facing aft on the bridge, his face grim with defiance, skilfully threw his ship from side to side, dodging the enemy's shells. On the poop, Hayter's gun's crew, who had fired only three practice shots since their gun was fitted, calmly returned shot for shot. In the engine-room, Chief Engineer Richard Parsons screwed down his boiler safety valves and advanced the engine control-lever hard up against the stops. The deep-loaded tramp rattled and vibrated until it seemed every rivet in her stout hull must pop. Abaft the bridge, in the tiny wireless cabin, the *Stonepool*'s radio officer, in the absence of any orders from the bridge, took it upon himself to tap out an unbroken call for help.

Soon the more accurate shooting of *U-42*'s 88 mm gun began to take its toll. The *Stonepool* was hit time and time again. Both her lifeboats were smashed, and with them went her crew's only hope of survival. They could only fight and run.

But *U-42* was not to have it all her own way. The *Stonepool*'s part-time gunners had at last found the range, and four-inch shells began to land uncomfortably close to the U-boat. In desperation, Dau fired a torpedo at the fleeing ship, but the canny Albert White was ready for this move. Watching the feathered track racing through the water towards the ship, he made a sharp alteration of course at the precise moment. The torpedo passed harmlessly down the starboard side and porpoised across the bows.

At the same time, one of Hayter's shells found its mark, and *U-42* crash-dived in a cloud of spray and smoke.

Ten minutes later the U-boat surfaced again, and White ordered his gunners to recommence firing. The submarine did not return the fire. Puzzled, White took the powerful ship's telescope from its rack and steadied it against an awning stanchion while he focused. When he lowered the telescope he was smiling. The U-boat's deck gun was pointing uselessly to the sky, its barrel smashed by one of the *Stonepool*'s shells. White's smile broadened when he noticed the U-boat steering an erratic course, as though she might be holed below the waterline.

Deciding that enough was enough, White broke off the action and steamed off to the west at all possible speed. Half an hour later, with the U-boat out of sight, he decided to resume the voyage and gave the order to alter course to the south. Unfortunately the *Stonepool* had taken more punishment than he realized. She had, in fact, been hit five times, some of the U-boat's shells striking near or below the waterline. A quick check on the bilges revealed she was making water in her holds. When Chief Officer Love reported that both lifeboats had been destroyed and the ship was settling by the head, White was obliged to reverse course and head back for the Bristol Channel.

About three hours later, at 15.00, the destroyers *Imogen* and *Ilex* appeared on the scene. The escorts had been on the point of turning for home following the dispersal of Convoy OB 17, when they picked up the *Stonepool*'s SOS. Racing to the position given by the *Stonepool*'s operator, they found *U-42* still on the surface and obviously crippled. They moved swiftly into the attack, but Kapitän-Leutnant Dau had no stomach left for the fight. He scuttled his boat, and he and his crew were taken prisoner by the destroyers. The career of *U-42* had been short and unproductive. In her only action of the war she had made the mistake of under-estimating the guts and capability of the crew of a British tramp and had paid the price.

As for the *Stonepool*, her ordeal was far from over. She was 450 miles from the nearest friendly port, badly knocked about and with the water rising in her holds. White's only consoling thought was that he had suffered no casualties in the engagement.

After disposing of *U-42*, *Imogen* and *Ilex* took station on the limping *Stonepool*, prepared to escort her back to port. However, the tramp was not to enjoy the comforting presence of the destroyers for long. At 17.00, when the setting sun was low in the west, the *Stonepool's* masthead look-out reported a submarine on the surface off the port beam. They were being shadowed again.

This time there was no need for the battered merchantman to fight a rearguard action. Her signal lamp winked out from the bridge, warning the escorts of the danger, and they peeled off to attack. The *Stonepool* was left to stagger home alone. She reached Barry on 16 October and lived to sail and fight another day. Her end finally came in the icy waters off Greenland in September 1941, when she was caught up in the dreadful massacre of Convoy SC 42. In an action lasting three days, a pack of ten U-boats, including *U-432*, commanded by the now legendary Herbert Schultze, destroyer of the *Heronspool*, sank sixteen merchantmen for the loss of only one of their number. Ironically, the U-boat lost, *U-207*, commanded by Oberleutnant Fritz Meyer, fell to the escorts' depth charges only a few hours after she had claimed her first, and only, victim of the war, the gallant *Stonepool*.

4   The One That Got Away

In the autumn of 1940, the whole of Western Europe lay supine under the iron heel of Hitler's Wehrmacht. Britain alone stood fast, but she was in mortal danger. Only the thin line of weather-beaten ships stretching across the North Atlantic to the arsenals and storehouses of the Americas could save her. But that lifeline was near to breaking. In September alone, sixty ships of 291,679 tons had fallen to the enemy, and the toll was rising steadily.

The situation was so when, in the early evening of 5 October, four U-boats slipped out of Lorient and turned their sleek, grey hulls to meet the Atlantic swells rolling in from the west. Led by Kapitän-Leutnant Fritz Frauenheim in *U-101*, the four boats were the outriders of the first of Admiral Dönitz's 'wolf packs', whose allotted task was finally and irrevocably to cut Britain's Atlantic lifeline. On that same day and within the hour, 2,360 miles to the west, Convoy SC 7 sailed from Sydney, Cape Breton, bound eastwards.

The majority of the thirty-five ships making up Convoy SC 7 were old, slow and, in some cases, woefully small. Many were plainly no match for the North Atlantic at the approach of winter and would normally have made the crossing only in high summer, if at all. But Britain's immediate needs were so great that the rewards on offer far outweighed the risks.

Fortunately the weather was fine and calm when SC 7 cleared the headlands of Sydney harbour and, with a great deal of black smoke and grumbling confusion, formed up into nine columns abreast and set off at its designated speed of seven knots. The convoy's meagre escort, consisting only of the 1,200-ton sloop HMS *Scarborough* and the Canadian armed yacht *Elk*, did not serve to inspire confidence in the breasts of the merchant

43

captains. Resolute though they might be, the naval ships were too small, too slow and too lightly armed to be a serious deterrent to the U-boats. If SC 7 was to arrive in British waters intact, it would need the protection of God and the luck of the Devil.

Leading the third column in the convoy was the British cargo ship *Blairspey*, commanded by fifty-four-year-old Captain James Walker of Glasgow. The *Blairspey*, a steamship of 4,155 tons, was owned by George Nisbet & Co of Glasgow, also known as the Clydesdale Navigation Company. Built in 1929, she was one of the younger and more agile members of SC 7, and for this reason Captain Walker had been appointed vice-commodore of the convoy. In addition to tending to his own ship, it was his task to assist the commodore, who flew his flag in the small Ellerman & Papyanni liner *Assyrian*, to mould together the motley collection of eighteen British, six Norwegian, four Greek, three Swedish, two Dutch, one French and one Danish merchantmen, in the hope that they would cross the ocean in some semblance of order. It was therefore with an added sense of pride that James Walker trod the bridge of his ship as they stood out into the Atlantic.

In her holds and on deck, the *Blairspey* carried a cargo of 1,798 standards of timber, loaded in Quebec for Grangemouth, on the Firth of Forth, a destination which pleased her mainly Scottish crew of thirty-four. They also took comfort from the fact that their full cargo of timber offered a degree of protection against the enemy. Should the *Blairspey* be torpedoed, she would almost certainly take a some time to go down, thereby giving her crew a chance to abandon ship in good order. It could not be said that the *Blairspey*'s armament offered such comfort. She carried only an ancient four-inch mounted on her poop and a .45 Thompson machine carbine on her bridge, a gun as incongruous in a British tramp as it was at home in the world of the Chicago gangsters.

The convoy's route, as laid down by the Admirality, would take it into the northernmost reaches of the Atlantic, to within 250 miles of Iceland, before then curving to the south-east to approach Britain through the North Channel, which runs between Ireland and Scotland. In this way, it was hoped to keep well out of range of patrolling U-boats until the final leg of the sixteen-day passage, at which point it was planned to reinforce the convoy's escort substantially.

Two days out of Sydney, the armed yacht *Elk* turned back for Nova Scotia, having reached the limit of her range. Fortunately for this diminutive warship, the weather up to this point had remained unusually calm. But as SC 7 inched its way to the west, with its sole escort, HMS *Scarborough*, bravely scouting ahead, the North Atlantic began to bare its teeth.

By the morning of the 11th, it was blowing a full gale from the north-west, which brought with it a heavy beam swell and rough, tumbling seas. Very soon, two of the smaller merchant ships, the 1,800-ton Great Lakes steamers *Trevisa* and *Eaglescliffe Hall*, were forced to drop out. It was indeed a miracle that those ships had progressed so far, for they had not been built for ocean steaming.

As the day wore on and the weather worsened, the bigger ships began to go. The first to fall back, wallowing helplessly in the troughs, was the 3,554-ton Greek vessel *Aenos*. She was quickly followed by her compatriot, the 5,875-ton *Thalia*. Both ships had suffered engine breakdowns, their old and poorly maintained machinery unable to stand up to the strain imposed by the heavy rolling and pitching.

The gale, which was part of a huge equinoctial depression moving across the North Atlantic, blew fiercely and without let-up for the next four days. Throughout, the remaining ships, although in some disarray, moved doggedly north-eastwards, with the gallant *Scarborough* rolling her rails under as she fought to provide a modicum of cover for her thirty-one charges. On the afternoon of the 15th, the *Aenos* rejoined and, coincident with her reappearance, the barometer began to rise, bringing a dramatic improvement in the weather. As the convoy was now less than twenty-four hours steaming from the rendezvous point with the local escort heading out from the North Channel, the prospects for a successful crossing began to look good.

The first intimation SC 7 had of approaching danger came in the darkest hours of the morning of the 16th, when distress calls were heard from the *Trevisa*. Straggling some 120 miles astern of the convoy, the small steamer had been torpedoed by *U-124*, one of the quartet of outriders that had left Lorient eleven days earlier. She had missed the main convoy and was casting about for victims to the west.

Sunset was only forty minutes away when, that afternoon, SC 7's luck ran out. *U-93*, commanded by Kapitän-Leutnant Klaus Korth, was patrolling on the surface when she sighted several columns of smoke on the horizon to the east. Pressing ahead at full speed, Korth was soon able to confirm his hopes: he had fallen in with a large British convoy. He reported his find to U-boat Headquarters at Lorient.

Dönitz ordered Korth to shadow the convoy, and then himself set about laying a foolproof trap. By midnight, a line of eight U-boats, led by the Admiral's top ace, Korvetten-Kapitän Otto Kretschmer, in *U-99*, was stretched across the path of the convoy.

Meanwhile help was at hand for SC 7. During the afternoon, HMS *Scarborough* had been joined by the sloop HMS *Fowey* and the Flower-class corvette HMS *Bluebell*, the first of the local escort to arrive. Between them, the three small warships still made up only a token show of force, but their mere presence indicated to the merchantmen that they were within striking distance of the safety of the North Channel. The morale of the convoy went up several notches.

On the bridge of the *Blairspey* that night the atmosphere was tense. Captain Walker and his officers were acutely aware that, if an attack was to be made on the convoy, it would happen within the next twenty-four hours. There had been many times during the crossing when Walker had roundly cursed the foul Atlantic weather, but now, with the wind and sea falling and a bright moon breaking through the clouds from time to time, he had an uneasy feeling in the pit of his stomach. Conditions for the U-boats could not have been better. Had Walker but known that the unseen shadower of the convoy, Klaus Korth in *U-93*, had been joined by Heinrich Bleichrodt in *U-48*, his uneasiness would have been even more acute.

The first hammer-blow fell at 03.00 on the morning of the 17th, when, on the instructions of Lorient, Heinrich Bleichrodt opened the attack. The 9,512-ton French tanker *Languedoc*, following close astern of the *Blairspey*, suddenly erupted in a sheet of flame. Seconds later, the 3,843-ton British cargo ship *Scoresby* sent distress rockets arching skywards as she was hit and began to sink. Bleichrodt's third torpedo caught and severely damaged the 4,678-ton *Haspenden*. Walker had little time to reflect on the horror of the sinkings, as the commodore had ordered a series of emergency turns. For a while confusion reigned in the hazard-filled darkness.

The remainder of the night passed without incident, and by dawn hope was once again rising in the now zigzagging ranks of the convoy. At 07.00 the escort was further reinforced by the Grimsby-class sloop HMS *Leith*, and a Sunderland flying-boat made a brief appearance overhead. Later in the day, another Flower-class corvette, HMS *Heartsease*, also joined. Even the sceptical Walker, bleary-eyed and unshaven after so many long hours on the bridge of the *Blairspey*, could see the odds on a safe arrival shortening.

It was with mixed feelings, therefore, that he watched the weather improving as the day wore on. Fine weather allowed a faster rate of advance towards safety, but it also meant more exposure to the seeking eyes of the enemy. By nightfall the visibility was excellent, with the moon behind the clouds shedding a diffused light on the columns of ships as they zigzagged across a calm sea. The five escorts, three sloops and two corvettes, were spread out around the perimeter of the convoy, their look-outs searching the horizon with night-glasses, asdics probing underwater. There was little else to be done but to wait and hope.

Shortly after 01.00 on the 18th, *U-38*, commanded by Kapitän-Leutnant Heinrich Liebe, penetrated the thin defensive screen from astern and sent a torpedo speeding towards the 3,670-ton British steamer *Carsbreck*, sailing in the outside column on the port side of the convoy. As the *Carsbreck*'s distress rockets flared, those on the bridge of the *Blairspey* caught sight of the track of another torpedo overtaking their ship on her port side. It was a near-miss but Walker did not take kindly to being shot at from astern. He felt doubly vulnerable.

The *Carsbreck* did not sink but her speed was greatly reduced and she began to straggle astern of the convoy. That she was still afloat was a stroke of good fortune for her crew, but it spelled disaster for the other ships when the corvette *Bluebell* was assigned to stand by her. In effect, Liebe had succeeded in reducing the convoy's escort by a substantial twenty per cent at one stroke.

By 19.00 the convoy had reached the furthest point north in its route and was 250 miles to the south of Iceland. The ships now altered course to the south-east, making for the entrance to the North Channel. The moon not yet being up, it was a black night and, with a little more than forty-eight hours to go before they came abreast of the Outer Hebrides and within range of continuous air cover, there were once more grounds for optimism. Then, without warning, the trap was sprung.

The first blow was dealt by Karl-Heinz Möhle in *U-123*, who torpedoed the 5,458-ton British ship *Shekatika*, which, being a timber-carrier, refused to sink. There was a lull of some forty minutes, then, just as it seemed the danger had receded, Engelbert Endrass in *U-46* and Fritz Frauenheim in *U-101* sank between them, in quick succession, the 4,885-ton Cardiff ship *Beatus*, the Swedish-flag *Convallaria* and the twenty-eight-year-old *Creekirk* of London.

For a while, confusion reigned. Distress rockets soared skywards, ship's whistles wailed and escorts dashed blindly to meet an enemy they could not see. In the midst of this, the commodore in the *Assyrian* and Walker in the *Blairspey* attempted to lead the ranks of nervous ships through a series of violent emergency turns. By the grace of God and the instinctive seamanship of the merchantmen, there were no collisions, and by 20.30 all was quiet again. The U-boats' score was now seven ships sunk and three damaged.

And the danger was not yet past, for Otto Kretschmer, in characteristic style, had maneouvred *U-99* into the middle of the convoy. His precisely aimed torpedo struck the largest ship in the convoy, the 6,055-ton *Empire Miniver*, sending her to the bottom. Twenty minutes later, quite coincidentally, Endrass in *U-46* sank the convoy's smallest ship, the 1,572-ton *Gunborg*.

Seeing the *Gunborg* go (she was only two ships astern of the *Blairspey*), Walker wondered how much time his own ship had left. All around him ships were sinking or disabled, and it was obvious that SC 7's puny escort force was powerless in the face of such a savage enemy. The temptation to cut and run was very great – to steam away from this awful nightmare at all possible speed, in the hope that safety might be found under cover of the night. But James Walker was too experienced a master to fall for the apparently easy option. He knew that, as soon as the

Blairspey strayed from the protection – dubious though it might be – of the convoy screen, the waiting wolves would pounce.

Even as Walker gave thought to his predicament, he heard from the starboard quarter the warning bellow of another ship's whistle. He ran to the starboard wing of the bridge and was in time to see the track of yet another torpedo overtaking his ship on a parallel course.

The convoy was now surrounded by U-boats, which were operating on the surface with impunity, for they outnumbered the hard-pressed escort ships of the Royal Navy by more than two to one. Circling the periphery and firing inwards were Heinrich Bleichrodt in *U-48*, Karl-Heinz Möhle in *U-123*, Engelbert Endrass in *U-46*, Fritz Frauenheim in *U-101*, Wilhelm Schulz in *U-124*, Heinrich Liebe in *U-38*, Joachim Schepke in *U-100* and Günter Kuhnke in *U-28*, while Otto Kretschmer cruised in the middle of the convoy firing outwards. Nine ships had gone, three others were damaged, and the slaughter was only just beginning.

The gods were surely on the side of the U-boats that night, for the heavy cloud-cover cleared away and the stricken convoy was bathed in the brilliant light of the full moon, now climbing high in the eastern sky.

A few minutes later, at 22.30, the *Blairspey* moved into the sights of *U-101*, and Fritz Frauenheim gave the order to fire. Walker felt rather than heard the dull thud. There was no eruption of smoke or flame, and for a few brief seconds he dared to hope that some other ship close at hand had been hit. Then the *Blairspey* staggered, a deluge of water rained down on the bridge and he knew the inevitable had happened.

Frauenheim's torpedo had struck the *Blairspey* in her No. 1 hold, about fifty feet from her bows. She took a slight list at first but quickly straightened up again. Then the air was suddenly filled with the roar of escaping high-pressure steam. The shock of the explosion had caused the blow-out of a joint in the main steam line to the engine. Robbed of their driving-force, the gleaming pistons of the *Blairspey*'s engine ground to a halt.

Soon the *Blairspey* was stopped and dead in the water, with the frightening cacophony of venting steam filling the night air around her. The rest of the convoy, intent on beating off its persistent attackers, was drawing slowly ahead. Walker felt very much alone and exposed. It was with some relief when, half an hour or so later, the senior escort ship, HMS *Leith*, appeared out of the darkness. The sloop circled the *Blairspey* and then came in close to enquire the extent of her damage. At this stage, Walker had no intention of abandoning his ship and informed the escort that he hoped to raise steam again and limp along in the rear of the convoy in company with the other damaged ships. *Leith* wished him luck and, with a flurry of foam at her stern, swept away to re-join the running battle.

The *Blairspey*'s chief engineer, Alexander Henderson, now took his men back into the steam-filled engine-room they had been forced to abandon. They were to spend the next two hours working without let-up to repack the blown joint.

Those on the bridge, who could only wait and watch, suffered a subtle torture of the most fiendish kind. As the convoy drew ahead and out of sight, so the moon went behind the clouds again and the darkness was complete. The uncanny silence was disturbed only by the slap of waves against the hull and the creak of derricks as they moved in their crutches with the roll of the ship. Each time the clang of a hammer rang out from deep in the engine-room, it was like the tolling of a funeral bell. Walker gritted his teeth, for he knew the job could not be done in silence.

For Henderson and his men, working by the light of flickering oil-lamps twenty feet below the waterline, the tension was even greater. Each time steel rang on steel or the curses grew loud, glances strayed to the thin hull plates, beyond which, in the silence of the deep, the enemy might be listening. The great, cathedral-like engine-space in which they worked with the sweat soaking into their boilersuits was the soft under-belly of the *Blairspey*. If a torpedo came crashing through those plates, there would be no escape for them.

Having been involved in the fierce battle of SC 7 for forty-eight hours without let-up, Joachim Schepke was tired. It was inevitable that when, at 01.00 on the 19th, he maneouvred *U-100* into position to deliver the *coup de grâce* to the helpless *Blairspey*, his judgement was flawed. He aimed for her engine-room but the torpedo struck between her No.1 and No.2 holds, which were packed tight with planks of Canadian timber.

The time had now come for Captain James Walker to make

that decision which haunts all who bear the burden of command of a ship. From the bridge, the effect of the second torpedo was much the same as that of the first. The dull thud, the shudder and the tall column of water thrown into the air were frightening but by no means fatal. While Walker was aware that the underwater plates of his ship were being savagely ripped open, he was confident her cargo would keep her afloat for many hours, perhaps days. However, he was a realist, and he knew it was only a matter of time before the U-boat, now using his crippled ship for target practice, put a torpedo into her engine-room. This, the largest single compartment in the ship, would flood rapidly, and that would be the end of the *Blairspey* – or would it? The ring of a hammer came again from the bowels of the ship, and Walker was reminded of his duty to those men below. He gave the order to abandon ship.

As is customary in a merchant ship, Walker, as master, took charge of the starboard lifeboat, while Chief Officer John Glasgow, an aptly named Glaswegian, had the port boat. Walker's boat, with twenty men on board, took the water smoothly and pulled clear. As Glasgow's boat was being lowered, Schepke put his second torpedo into the *Blairspey*, which exploded directly below the suspended boat.

Believing his chief officer and his boat's crew had been killed, Walker took his own boat away from the *Blairspey*. A few minutes later, both *U-101* and *U-100* approached the lifeboat and asked for the name of the ship. The U-boats seemed to be cruising on the surface with complete disregard of any danger to themselves, which was understandable, for the convoy and its escort were now out of sight over the horizon. The Germans, obviously believing the *Blairspey* would sink of her own accord, made no attempt to shell or torpedo her again.

Being of much the same opinion as the U-boat commanders, Walker took one last, lingering look at his command and prepared to set sail for the Irish coast, which lay a hundred miles to the south-west. As the sails were being hoisted, he was greatly relieved to see the other lifeboat appear out of the darkness. By some miracle, Glasgow and his men had survived the torpedo uninjured and without damage to their boat.

During what remained of the night, the wind freshened, bringing with it a choppy sea, and the two lifeboats became separated. Soon after dawn, Walker and his men were picked up by the corvette *Bluebell*, which already had on board 150 survivors from various ships. John Glasgow and his men were not so fortunate. It was late afternoon before they were rescued by a salvage tug.

For Convoy SC 7 the one-sided fight had continued throughout the night. Before the grey light of dawn came on the 19th, another five ships had been lost. Only then did the U-boats withdraw, some to return in triumph to Lorient, others to attack Convoy HX 79, which was approaching from the west. There they would add another twelve ships to their score.

Early on the morning of the 20th, the Atlantic took a final, spiteful swipe at SC 7: a howling gale, accompanied by blinding rainstorms, scattering the tattered remnants of the convoy. Sanctuary was eventually found in the sheltered waters of the Firth of Clyde on the 21st, but of the thirty-five ships that had set out from Canada sixteen days before, only fifteen remained.

So ended one of the bloodiest battles in recent maritime history. The U-boats, operating on the surface at night, had been able to run rings around the slow, lightly armed escorts of SC 7. Confused and defenceless, the merchant ships were been picked off at will. In the space of seventy-two hours, twenty ships, totalling 79,646 tons, went to the bottom, and with them went over 100,000 tons of precious cargo and several hundred merchant seamen. The heaviest slaughter took place on the night of 18/19 October, which thereafter became known amongst the U-boat men as 'The Night of the Long Knives'.

One of the great ironies of the battle of Convoy SC 7 was that the tiny *Eaglescliffe Hall*, which had dropped out of the convoy shortly after sailing from Sydney, found her way across the Atlantic alone and unprotected. On her way, she picked up twenty-five survivors from the torpedoed Greek steamer *Aenos*, thereby playing a valuable role in the operation.

As for the *Blairspey*, in spite of the three torpedoes she had suffered, she lived to sail another day. When the shooting stopped, she was found still afloat and towed into the Clyde by a deep-sea tug.

U-101 survived the war and was surrendered to British forces in May 1945. *U-100* did not have the same good fortune. On 17 march 1941 she was caught on the surface while attacking

Convoy HX 112 and rammed and sunk by the destroyer HMS *Vanoc*. Joachim Schepke and all but five of his crew went down with her.

5   The Other Enemy

For the men of Britain's tramp ships, winter in the North Atlantic had never been anything but a season of acute discomfort and danger. To spend day after day and night after sleepless night hove-to with green seas sweeping the decks, cabins awash and muscles aching through constant bracing against the roll and pitch of a ship in torment was accepted as an occupational hazard. Frequently these slow and deeply laden ships limped into port with lifeboats reduced to matchwood, hatches leaking and coal-bunkers all but empty. Occasionally one of their number would be lost without trace, simply overwhelmed by the awesome power of an angry sea that knew no bounds for a thousand miles in any direction. This too was accepted.

The winter of 1940 was said to be the worst ever recorded in the North Atlantic. It was a time when a never-ending series of deep depressions marched across that wide expanse of ocean, each following so close on the heels of the other that the barometer appeared to be stuck at an all-time low for months on end. Rarely did the wind drop below gale force, and often it rose to such a screaming crescendo that even the most hardened Western Ocean men found butterflies stirring in their stomachs. The long Atlantic rollers became great, white-topped mountains that sought to brush the low-hanging clouds and hid dark valleys deep enough to swallow a 5,000-ton ship from truck to keel.

To all this, in 1940, was added the constant threat of the skulking U-boat and the shadowy surface raider. The silent torpedo could break a ship's back like the punch of a sharp-fanged reef, and the whistling, long-range shell make a bloody shambles of an unprotected bridge and its occupants. And now there was yet another enemy to face.

Following the fall of France, in June 1940, and the subsequent availability of new bases on the Biscay coast, Hitler decided to strengthen the U-boat arm by the use of reconnaissance aircraft to seek out Allied shipping. For this role the four-engined Focke-Wulf Condor was chosen. The Condor had a range of over 2,000 miles and a top speed of 224 mph, carried a bomb-load of 4,626 pounds and was armed with a formidible array of machine-guns and cannon. Flying from an operational base set up near Bordeaux, the Condors very quickly proved to be invaluable as the 'eyes' of the U-boats, and their progression to the attacking role was inevitable. Although this great, lumbering aircraft was too vulnerable to approach an escorted convoy, it proved remarkably effective against the lone merchantman.

On Saturday 26 October 1940 Convoy OB 235 sailed from the deep-water harbour of Milford Haven and headed west into St George's Channel. The barometer was falling steadily and, under a lowering cloud base, the white horses had begun to gallop. At this stage, OB 235 consisted of only a handful of ships and was lightly escorted. Later, off Liverpool, and later still off the Firth of Clyde, other ships would join and the escort would be reinforced before the completed convoy passed through the North Channel and out into the Atlantic.

In the ranks of the embryo OB 235 as it cleared the Welsh coast was the 5,702-ton steamer *Starstone*, owned by the Alva Steamship Company of London. Commanded by forty-three-year-old Captain W.R. Thomas of Cardiff, she was a comparatively new ship, having been built by William Doxford & Sons at Sunderland only a year before the outbreak of war. However, like most tramps of her day, she was lamentably underpowered. On her trials, light ship and under ideal conditions, she had achieved a speed of ten knots. Deep-loaded and with a perpetually dirty bottom through lack of dry-docking, her performance was, to say the least, unimpressive. On her current voyage she was, as usual, riding low in the water, down to her marks with 8,500 tons of coal, loaded at Barry for the River Plate.

In the less regimented days of peace, when merchant ships were free to go their own separate ways without interference from admirals and enemies, Captain Thomas would have taken a south-westerly course after leaving the Bristol Channel: once clear of the Bay of Biscay, some three days later, the worst of the Atlantic weather would then have been behind him. Unfortunately on this voyage the logical and time-honoured route to South America was not open to him. As a result of the capitulation of France and the occupation of her long Atlantic coastline by German forces, the Admiralty had laid a huge minefield across the south-western approaches to Britain. St George's Channel and the English Channel were completely sealed off, so that the only access to and from all ports lay to the north. The *Starstone* would be forced to go out through the North Channel, between Ireland and Scotland. Apart from adding 800 miles to her passage, this northern route took the ship directly into the path of the fiercest Atlantic gales for two days longer than normally necessary. Given that his ship was very deep-laden, with precious little freeboard, this gave Thomas grounds for concern.

As far as the dangers presented by the enemy were concerned, Thomas felt rather more confident. In addition to the usual four-inch anti-submarine gun, the *Starstone* also mounted on her poop a twelve-pounder anti-aircraft gun, and on her bridge a Hotchkiss .303 machine-gun. As a morale-booster more than anything else, Thomas also kept a .303 rifle to hand in the wheel-house. The *Starstone* carried only one DEMS gunner, Gunlayer Jackson of the Royal Navy, who had organized and trained guns' crews from the ship's officers and ratings. The only weak link in the *Starstone*'s defence, in Thomas's opinion, lay in her unprotected wheel-house. It had not yet been shielded with concrete armour, as was the normal practice in merchant ships at this stage of the war, it being realized that the vital control centre of the ship must be, at least, proof against bullets and flying shrapnel. Yet, in spite of Thomas's persistent lobbying of the relevant authorities at each port visited, the *Starstone* had sailed from Barry with her wheel-house unprotected.

Thomas might also have been forgiven if he had anticipated crew problems on this voyage, for his men were certainly one of the most cosmopolitan assemblies ever to sail out of Britain in one ship. While Thomas and his chief engineer were Cardiff men, his chief officer hailed from County Durham, his second officer from Glasgow, his third officer from Norway, his first radio officer from Swaziland, his fourth engineer from South Africa and his chief steward, who bore the fairy-tale name of Hans Christian Olsen, was a native of Denmark. In the forecastle, the carpenter was Japanese, the deck crew were from Sierra Leone, the engine-room ratings from India, and the stewards were British. As subsequent events were to prove, no better prototype for the as yet unformed United Nations could have been found anywhere.

At noon on the 28th the convoy, having trailed its coat across the estuaries of the Mersey and Clyde, had swollen to thirty-three ships and was passing the Mull of Kintyre, bound out through the North Channel. The naval escort consisted of the destroyers *Veteran*, *Verity*, *Chelsea* and *Witherton* and the Flower-class corvette *Gentian*. But this seemingly generous protective screen was short-term, as OB 235 was to disperse 300 miles to the west of Ireland.

The *Starstone* was the leading ship in the third column and was for the moment, comfortably maintaining the convoy speed of eight knots. The weather was fine, with only a slight sea running, and there was a crisp, exhilarating bite in the air which spoke of the winter soon to come. On the bridge of the *Starstone*, Captain Thomas turned up the collar of his bridgecoat and regarded the weather with suspicion. Winter in the North Atlantic was all very well for some, but he would not rest easy until he felt the Portuguese Trades on his back, safe in the knowledge that it was all fair-weather sailing from then on.

On deck, Chief Officer H.L. Poulson's thoughts were also running ahead of the ship. At twenty-eight Poulson was comparatively young to be in such a senior position, but he had learned his trade in a hard school. At the head of his long list of shipboard responsibilities was the care of the *Starstone*'s cargo of coal. To the uninitiated, the carriage of this dirty and apparently inert cargo might appear undemanding, but Poulson, through past experience, knew better.

The transportation of coal in ships is fraught with the dangers of fire and explosion, and over the years many a fine vessel has been lost as a result. Immediately after loading, coal emits an inflammable gas, which can explode with catastrophic results on contact with a spark or naked flame. Consequently maximum ventilation is required during the early stages of the voyage, even to the extent of leaving open corner hatchboards, a practice which calls for a careful eye on the weather. The risk of fire is longer-term and usually caused by spontanteous combustion taking place deep in the cargo when too much oxygen is absorbed from the air. In this case, excessive ventilation increases the risk. So, in caring for a cargo of coal at sea, a thin tightrope must be walked. Insufficient ventilation may result in an explosion, whereas too much air flowing into the holds could well start and fuel a deep-seated fire which is almost impossible to extinguish at sea.

All the 'alarums and excursions' of war apart, Poulson had much to occupy his mind on the long passage to the River Plate.

Soon after the convoy rounded the north of Ireland, the wind began to freshen, and by the early hours of the morning of the 29th a full gale was blowing from the west. Before dawn, the *Starstone*'s Japanese carpenter, W. Wada, was on deck in oilskins and sea-boots hastily battening down the corner hatches. Chief Officer Poulson's careful attention to the ventilation of the cargo had come to naught. The sea was now presenting a greater danger to the ship than pockets of marsh gas.

Throughout that morning the wind continued to strengthen, and by noon it reached storm force. The *Starstone*, sitting low in the water, found her decks being swept by angry green seas as she struggled valiantly to keep up with the convoy. But, despite Chief Engineer Cusworth's careful nursing of his engine, she was soon down to six knots and falling astern of the other ships. When the davits of her port lifeboat were bent and her jollyboat smashed by huge seas, Thomas decided that enough was enough. Much to the relief of his harassed chief engineer, he called for reduced revolutions and pulled the *Starstone* out of the convoy. Very soon she was alone on the storm-swept sea.

For the next thirty-six hours, the *Starstone* was hove to with with wind and sea on the bow, her engines giving the slowest possible speed compatible with steerageway. Her forward progress was negligible, but she was able to ride out the mountainous seas without taking any more grievous punishment. That she was a sitting duck for any U-boat that might happen along, Thomas refused to contemplate. For the time being, his most pressing enemy was the sea.

By dawn on the 21st, when the *Starstone* was 200 miles west of Ireland, the wind had eased to gale force, and it was possible to increase speed to five knots. There was still a heavy sea running and the cloud was low, but visibility was beginning to improve, indicating that the depression was passing. Thomas saw little hope of rejoining the other ships but, feeling that the effort was required of him, set a course calculated to intercept the convoy.

At 09.15, when the cloud had lifted still further, an aircraft was sighted approaching from the south-west. Thomas was on the bridge with twenty-nine-year-old Third Officer Hansen, who had the watch. Both men lifted their binoculars at the look-out's warning shout, located and focused on the black dot low down on the horizon. Thomas was no expert at aircraft-recognition, but he realized at once that this was no friendly Sunderland swooping in to pay its respects. He ordered Hansen to sound action stations.

Before the alarm bells had stopped ringing, Gunlayer Jackson, with Chief Steward Olsen hard at his heels, was racing aft to the twelve-pounder. Behind them, at a more sedate pace, came the Sierra Leonian seamen who made up the rest of the gun's crew.

On the bridge, Second Officer Joseph Kelly, who had just arrived to take his morning sun-sight, put down his sextant and slammed a magazine into the Hotchkiss. He tested the gun with a quick burst to seaward.

In the wheel-house, the helmsman, Able Seaman George Taylor, gripped the spokes of the wheel tightly and wondered how on earth he had allowed himself to get mixed up in this white man's war.

Tumbling out through the galley door, clutching a half-eaten bacon sandwich, sixteen-year-old cabin-boy Ernest Webb rushed to the ship's side rail and gazed in awe at the approaching plane. On his first voyage to sea, he was determined not to miss a move in the drama.

Captain Thomas watched tight-lipped as the aircraft banked and flew down the port side of the ship at a distance of about two miles. He was unable to make out any markings, but the squarish wing tips, the gondola-like structure under the fuselage and the irregular beat of the four engines were characteristics too ominous to ignore. He passed the word to the wireless-room to send out an 'AAA' signal, indicating that the ship was under attack by enemy aircraft.

The plane flew on past the ship, then tipped its wings to port and came around in a tight circle to end up head into the wind and right astern. For a while it seemed to hover in the wake of the ship, as though the pilot was deliberating on how to begin the attack. By this time Thomas could see quite plainly the black crosses on the underside of the aircraft's wings. He gave the order to open fire with the twelve-pounder.

On the gun-platform aft, Olsen set the fuse on the first shell to 1,250 yards and nodded confidently to Gunlayer Jackson. The breech clanged shut and the gun barked. A puff of black smoke appeared close to the tail of the Focke-Wulf. Olsen shortened the next fuse to 750 yards, Jackson adjusted his sights, and the second round burst only yards off the plane's nose. For a gun which had seen better days, manned by a largely untrained crew, this was excellent shooting.

But if the German pilot was at all worried by the *Starstone*'s spirited defence, he failed to show it. The Focke-Wulf roared down the starboard side of the ship at mast-top height with all its guns blazing.

Second Officer Kelly opened fire with the Hotchkiss, but the gun jammed after a few rounds and he was left cursing impotently as he tried to clear the fouled breech. Captain Thomas, who was crouching in the wing of the bridge with his .303 rifle, jumped up as the plane came abeam and took aim. The loud roar of the plane's engines, the hammering of her machine-guns and the crack of the twelve-pounder, all intermingled with the howling wind – for the gale was still blowing, produced a frightening discord. But Thomas, furious at this unprovoked attack on his ship and oblivious to the bullets thudding into the wooden deck beneath his feet, returned the enemy's fire as fast as he could work the bolt of his rifle. So occupied was he that he failed to notice the helmsman, George Taylor, who had been crouching at his side, go down with a bullet in his eye.

The Focke-Wulf swept past the bridge, with its rear turret opening up to add to the mad symphony. Thomas, who was busy reloading, saw an ominous shape fall away from under the plane's wing.

The bomb landed on the starboard side of the forecastle head, bounced over the anchor cables and exploded on the port side of the deck with a crash that shook the *Starstone* from stem to stern. When the smoke cleared, Thomas looked down from the bridge on a scene of devastation. The forward bulwarks were shattered, the windlass had been torn from its mountings, and black smoke poured from the paint-locker.

With the helm unattended, the ship's head was now falling off and there was danger of her broaching to in the heavy seas. At a word from Thomas, Taylor, although blind in one eye and with blood running down his face, returned to the wheel and brought the ship back up into the wind.

The next attack came from ahead, the Focke-Wulf again flying down the starboard side. The twelve-pounder opened up, Thomas crouched low with his .303 at the ready, but Kelly was still desperately trying to clear his jammed Hotchkiss.

This time the German pilot, possibly disconcerted by the fierce opposition, miscalculated, and his second bomb fell into the sea off the *Starstone*'s starboard quarter. He circled and came in from astern, but again the bomb exploded harmlessly in the sea.

The plane now took a wide, deliberate sweep before returning to the attack for the fourth time, approaching from dead ahead. This time there was no mistake. The bomb landed on the after-deck abreast of No.4 hatch, penetrating the steel deck before exploding. Hatchboards, beams and tarpaulins were hurled skywards, derricks and winches crumpled and the *Starstone*'s mainmast slowly keeled over and collapsed into the open hatchway. Within a few moments, tongues of flames and billows of black smoke could be seen coming from the hatchway. The Focke-Wulf now withdrew and began to circle well out of range.

Thomas lowered his smoking rifle and called for a damage report. He found his ship was on fire fore and aft and extensively damaged on deck. The wireless aerials had been shot away and the transmitter wrecked. No.4 hold was making water, indicating that the hull had been breached. Bearing in mind the inflammable nature of his cargo and the fact that the fire aft was dangerously close to the ammunition lockers, Thomas reluctantly decided his ship might not have long to go.

Fortunately the weather was now moderating rapidly, so he ordered that the one serviceable lifeboat be lowered and sent away in charge of Second Officer Kelly with twenty of the older and less able of the crew. The Focke-Wulf, evidently satisfied the *Starstone* was being abandoned, flew away to the south-east.

Those who stayed on board to tackle the fires were Thomas himself, Chief Officer Poulson, Third Officer Hansen, Chief Engineer Cusworth, Second Engineer Riley and the young cabin-boy Ernest Webb. Hoses were rigged and within an hour the ship was out of danger. The lifeboat was recalled and Thomas prepared to get under way again, making for the north coast of Ireland, where he intended to beach the ship if she showed any sign of sinking.

The defence the *Starstone* had put up against a vastly superior enemy spoke volumes for the determination and courage of Captain Thomas and his cosmopolitan crew. Throughout the action, although bullets, cannon-shells and bombs had rained down on them, not one man had flinched from his duty. The scratch gun's crew of the twelve-pounder had loaded and fired with a coolness and precision that had had a marked deterrent effect on the Focke-Wulf. It was unfortunate that the Hotchkiss had jammed, but Kelly had never given up trying to clear the gun, even though he was under fire from the air. Thomas, completely oblivious to danger, had defended his bridge with the .303 until the enemy came no more. Above all, there had been no sign of panic. It was as though the *Starstone*'s men – culled from the four corners of the earth and many of them owing no real loyalty to the flag their ship flew – had regarded the attack as a very personal thing.

During the Focke-Wulf's first attack, Chief Steward Hans Christian Olsen, breech-worker on the twelve-pounder, had taken a machine-gun bullet in his arm. He was eventually persuaded to leave the gun to have his wound dressed but was caught on deck when the plane swooped in again and was shot through the neck. Olsen, a naturalized Briton who had lived in Cardiff for over thirty years, died with his face to the enemy responsible for the rape of the country of his birth.

Gunlayer Jackson, whose expertise with the twelve-pounder was probably responsible for the Focke-Wulf's not pressing home the attack with more determination, had ended the action with three enemy bullets in his body but still at his post. George Taylor, far from his native Freetown and with a bullet in his eye, had gone back to the wheel and stayed there until he collapsed from loss of blood. The Japanese carpenter, Wada, a man who knew no home but the *Starstone*, had been shot in the knee and must have been in great agony but did not complain; it was not until the day after the action that Thomas discovered that the Japanese was wounded. South African-born Fourth Engineer Peter Johnson, on his first trip to sea, had shown exceptional bravery in sticking to his post in the engine-room despite the bombs. Third Officer Hansen, in the opinion of Captain Thomas, had been a tower of strength throughout, not only physically but inspirationally, to all on board. And there was the cabin-boy, Ernest Webb, little more than a schoolboy, who in the space of a few short hours had moved into courageous manhood.

During the action three others had been injured, including twenty-eight-year-old Third Engineer Andrew Lloyd Smith, who was in a very serious condition.

The *Starstone* had been under way again for only a few hours when she was overtaken by the British armed merchant cruiser *Alcantara*, which had rushed to her aid on hearing her 'AAA' signal. The AMC offered to escort the damaged steamer into port, but Thomas refused the offer, insisting that his ship was capable of making her own way. He later admitted that his decision was influenced by reports he had received earlier of U-boats in the area. He was loath to put the 22,000-ton ex-Royal Mail liner and her large crew at risk while playing nursemaid to a limping tramp.

On the morning of 1 November the *Starstone* was in the North Channel and heading for the Clyde at all possible speed. Thomas, tired and drawn, still paced the bridge, but there was a new confidence in his walk. It seemed that the long nightmare would soon be over. Then the drone of aircraft engines drifted across the water, and the adrenalin began to run again.

Before the plane could be indentified as British, the twelve-pounder gun's crew was in position and ready to fire, with Second Officer Kelly acting gunlayer in place of the injured Jackson. When the familiar roundels of the RAF were recognized, there was almost an air of anti-climax at the gun. On

Wartime-built merchantman battling against storm-force winds in far northern waters.

Russia-bound convoy steaming through 'Arctic sea smoke'. This low-lying fog forms in fine weather where the warm flow of the Gulf Stream meets and mixes with cold Arctic water.

s.s. *Harmatris* 5395 GRT (gross registered tonnage) in her peacetime livery.

Convoy assembling in Milford Haven. The barrage balloons were flown to deter low-flying enemy aircraft.

A quiet moment for the Second Mate during the middle watch.

s.s. *Inishtrahull* 869 GRT, a typical coastal collier of the late 1930s.

Top: m.v. *Larchbank* 5150 GRT, one of Andrew Weir's worldwide traders.
Centre: s.s. *Treworlas* 4992 GRT, an elegant old ship of the Hain Line.
Bottom: s.s. *Heronspool* 5202 GRT, one of Sir Robert Ropner's best.

Veteran merchant seaman on DEMS gunnery course tries his hand
with a Hotchkiss machine-gun.

Torpedoed petroleum tanker goes up in flames.

Convoy puts up fierce anti-aircraft barrage when attacked from the air.

Long-range Liberator of Coastal Command watches over a tanker in the Western Approaches.

Journey's end: survivors coming alongside a rescue ship.

s.s. *Starstone* 5702 GRT, a typical Bristol Channel tramp.

North Atlantic convoy in nine columns of five with escorts scouting ahead. An example of station-keeping at its best.

orders from the bridge, Kelly secured the twelve-pounder, and the crew went forward to the accommodation, their shoulders drooping with fatigue but with pride in their eyes. On their way forward they met Jackson crawling along the deck towards his gun. Despite his wounds and the loss of blood he had suffered, the naval gunner had been determined to get to his post when the alarm bells sounded. It took four men to carry him, protesting vigorously, back to his cabin.

At 14.00 on the 1st, in sight of the brooding island of Arran which stands sentinel over the entrance to the Firth of Clyde, Third Engineer Andrew Lloyd Smith died of his wounds.

The battered *Starstone* arrived at Greenock later that afternoon. There were no cheering crowds or rousing brass bands to welcome her, only a doctor to tend her injured and a bowler-hatted dockyard superintendent to survey her many scars. When repairs were discussed, the first priority on Captain Thomas's list went to the fitting of armour to the bridge and a shield to the twelve-pounder. In view of the weight of evidence he now had to present, one must presume that this time he won his case.

6   The Inishtrahull and the Bomb

In peace or in war, life aboard a small collier is invariably hard, uncomfortable and unglamorous. The mechanized loading of coal makes for quick turn-arounds in port and, while passages between ports are also short, they are often nightmare battles against the hostile elements. And then there is the cargo. The carriage of coal is attended by a considerable risk, stemming from the presence of methane gas explosions and deep-seated fires caused by spontaneous combustion being quite common in a loaded collier. Added to this, the every-present coal dust, disturbed during loading or discharging, deposits a black film on every exposed surface and, despite securely battened ports and doors, permeates into the very heart of the accommodation. Everything a man touches, eats or drinks is contaminated by this gritty curse. Little wonder the men who crew the coastal colliers are a tough, resourceful breed.

The *Inishtrahull*, of 869 tons gross, was a typical small coal-carrier of her day. Built in 1935 by John Lewis & Sons of Aberdeen and owned by John Kelly Ltd of Queen's Quay, Belfast, she was a steamship 198 feet long and thirty-one feet in the beam, with a reputed top speed of eleven knots. Her engine-room and main accommodation were set right aft, leaving space on her foredeck for two large hatchways, through which her grimy cargo was worked. Separating the two hatchways was a small bridge-house, topped by a flimsy wooden wheel-house. Her funnel was tall and thin, and she sported three raked masts, the forward two each supporting a single derrick served by a steam winch on deck.

In grudging acknowledgement of the dangers of war, the *Inishtrahull* mounted a .303 Hotchkiss machine-gun in each wing of her bridge, and on her after deck she carried a Holman

Projector, the only 'secret weapon' ever to be entrusted to British merchant seamen. The Holman Projector was in fact a crude form of mortar which used steam under pressure to fire hand-grenades at low-flying aircraft. Its performance was more spectacular than effective and, as the supply of deck steam in a merchant ship is, to say the least, somewhat erratic, the grenades often had a disturbing tendency to fall back on deck after being fired. The operator of a Holman Projector therefore, in addition to possessing nerves of steel, was required to be fleet of foot. In the case of the *Inishtrahull*, this was Seaman Gunner William Gregg, the ship's sole DEMS rating.

Commanded by forty-two-year-old Captain Robert Gibson of County Antrim and carrying a total crew of fourteen, the *Inishtrahull* left the port of Limerick, on the west coast of Ireland, on the evening of 12 March 1942, bound in ballast for Ayr, in the Firth of Clyde. Her route would take her around the north of Ireland and through the North Channel, a distance of 427 miles. Gibson planned to be alongside the berth in Ayr in time for the morning shift on the 14th.

The mouth of the River Shannon was cleared by midnight, and the *Inishtrahull* entered the open sea and settled down on a north-north-westerly course with the Irish coast on her starboard beam. It was a black night – the moon having not yet risen – but the wind was light and the sea relatively calm. While this would make for a comfortable passage, which was to be welcomed, Gibson could not help sniffing suspiciously at the air as he watched the twinkling lights of neutral Ireland passing to starboard. He was only too well aware that on this coast light winds and a nip in the air often meant that fog was not far away. In fact, he could already smell the unmistakeable salty dampness. By dawn, he estimated, it would be as thick as a hedge and likely to stay that way, turning the rest of the passage around the treacherous, tide-swept coast into a navigator's nightmare. In common with most of her contemporaries, the collier's only navigational aids were a magnetic compass and a keen-eyed look-out.

But the rest of the night passed fine and clear, and the *Inishtrahull* pressed northwards at full speed. When dawn came, she was off the coast of Connemara, and although it had become hazy, Gibson's expectations of dense fog were not realized. On reflection, he would have felt more at ease if his gloomy prediction had proved right, for his small ship, alone on a neutral coast, was now dangerously exposed to the eyes of the enemy.

At ten o'clock that morning, the *Inishtrahull* was 1½ miles to the south-west of Eagle Island and less than a day's run from Ayr. Once round the island, she would come onto a north-easterly course to run across the broad sweep of Donegal Bay, picking up the coast again off Tory Island. From there it was a mere four hours steaming to pass abeam of the island of Inishtrahull, for which the ship was named. She would then enter the North Channel, where she would come under the protective umbrella of the Royal Navy and Coastal Command, who patrolled this northern gateway to Britain with great assiduity.

When, at 10.10, a large, four-engined aircraft was sighted on the *Inishtrahull*'s starboard quarter, approaching from over the land, Gibson assumed the RAF had arrived on the scene rather earlier than usual. He focused his binoculars and peered at the aircraft through the haze. She had the look of a Sunderland flying boat, and yet … The plane flew closer, crossing astern of the ship, and Gibson's stomach turned over. The visitor was a German Focke-Wulf Condor, the black crosses showing up clearly on her camouflaged fuselage. Gibson reached for the whistle lanyard.

As would be expected in a ship with only fourteen crew and armed with two light machine-guns and a grenade-thrower, 'action stations' in the *Inishtrahull* was an uncomplicated and expedient operation. Gibson was immediately joined on the bridge by his two deck officers, First Mate Samuel Dalzell and Second Mate Wilfred Hosier; Chief Engineer William Roberts and Second Engineer Neale Mitchell went below, and Seaman Gunner William Gregg sprinted aft to his Holman Projector. The rest of the crew took cover.

The Focke-Wulf banked steeply and then approached from astern, flying at about 400 feet above the sea. Gibson instructed Dalzell to take over the bridge and stationed himself at the Hotchkiss in the starboard wing. As was his prerogative and his nature, he intended to take a very active part in the defence of his ship. In the port wing of the bridge, thirty-seven-year-old

Wilfred Hosier, as tenacious as his Liverpool birthplace, prepared to do the same. On the poop, Seaman Gunner Gregg carefully removed the safety-pin from a hand-grenade and slipped the bomb into the cigarette-tin-like cylinder that would hold the firing-handle in place until the missile was thrown into the air.

On Captain Gibson's orders, fire was held until the aircraft had closed to about 400 yards. Then he squeezed the trigger of his Hotchkiss, aiming at the nose of the Focke-Wulf. Hosier, in the port wing, joined in, but his gun jammed after half a dozen rounds had been fired. As the plane drew closer, its gun turrets spitting fire, Seaman Gunner Gregg dropped his grenade into the muzzle of the Holman Projector, took aim and jerked the lever that released the high-pressure steam into the barrel. Much to his surprise, the crude gun functioned perfectly, hurling the grenade in its restraining tin high into the air right in the path of the approaching aircraft. Again, as per manual, the tin fell away at 300 feet, and the grenade continued its ascent for another three or four seconds before exploding. It was a hundred feet too high.

Unharmed, the Focke-Wulf roared in, its bomb doors gaping wide and preceded by a swathe of bullets and cannon-shells from its six gun positions, which sprayed the decks of the *Inishtrahull*, working from aft to forward. Wilfred Hosier, cursing loudly as he struggled to clear his gun, felt the wind of the thousand-pound bomb as it sliced past. The bomb struck the bridge rail less than six feet away from him but fortunately failed to explode and shot harmlessly into the sea.

On the other side of the bridge, Gibson's Hotchkiss was working faultlessly, and as the great, menacing shape roared overhead, its engines filling the air with the scream of a thousand angry demons, he poured a full belt of ammunition into its exposed underbelly.

The pilot of the Focke-Wulf, obviously shaken by the spirited defence put up by the little ship, flew on almost to the horizon before banking and then flying down the starboard side of the *Inishtrahull*, well out of reach of her guns. Once astern, he banked again and dropped to 150 feet above the water before beginning his second run.

Once again Gibson and his men stood to their guns, steeling

themselves as the enemy's forward gun turrets rattled into action, striking fire from the decks of their ship. When the Focke-Wulf was within range, Gregg got off another grenade from his projector, and Gibson and Hosier opened fire simultaneously. Hosier's gun again jammed after a few rounds but Gibson kept firing. He watched with grim satisfaction as his tracers struck home in the fuselage of the attacking plane, then his own gun also jammed. As the Focke-Wulf swooped over, he noted that its lower, rear turret appeared to be out of action, possibly hit during the first attack.

Gibson also saw the second bomb fall away from the Focke-Wulf's bomb-bay as the plane flashed by only a few feet above the collier's mainmast. He gave up his attempts to clear the Hotchkiss and watched transfixed as the bomb slammed into the forecastle head, only fifty feet forward of the bridge. Miraculously, this bomb also failed to explode on impact, but Gibson's relief turned to fear when the bomb rolled slowly down the deck, smashed through the rails at the break of the forecastle head and fell to the maindeck. To add to his present difficulties, Gibson now had an unexploded thousand-pound bomb lying within spitting distance of the bridge. Better men would have panicked in such a situation.

But there was no time for panic or for deliberation on the luck of the Irish, for the Focke-Wulf, having circled again, was now coming up astern once more. Both Gibson and Hosier had succeeded in clearing their guns and kept up a continuous fire as the plane swooped in for its bombing run. Seaman Gunner Gregg painstakingly aimed and fired his projector, but the grenade again burst too high. However, the German pilot now seemed to have lost his nerve, for he dropped his bomb 150 feet short of the ship and sheered off, but not before the two Hotchkiss guns had raked the plane with a full belt apiece.

This bomb exploded on contact with the sea, sending up a tall column of grey-green water. The blast swept across the *Inishtrahull* like a localized hurricane, shaking the small ship and sending loose equipment hurtling in all directions. Gibson was hit by a flying cargo block and thrown from his gun.

By the time the Focke-Wulf had circled and embarked on its fourth attack, approaching from astern as before, Gibson, nursing a badly bruised arm, was back at his gun. He sprayed the plane with a full belt as it thundered in. Hosier was able to fire only fifteen rounds before his troublesome Hotchkiss again jammed, and Gregg experienced the recurring frustration of seeing his missile explode harmlessly above the attacking aircraft. This time the enemy's bomb fell some 150 feet ahead of the *Inishtrahull*, shaking her but causing no damage.

It seemed that there was to be no end to this one-sided battle, for the Focke-Wulf had tipped her wings and was coming in for the fifth time. The indefatigable Gregg fired his steam-powered mortar but, as on the previous occasions, the grenade burst in thin air. Gibson and Hosier held their fire until the plane was almost overhead, and both got off full belts, hosing the underside of the wings and fuselage with tracer. The Focke-Wulf replied with cannon and machine-guns, two cannon-shells bursting in the starboard wing of the collier, wounding Gibson in the chest and shoulders.

The bomb was a very near miss, falling only a hundred feet off the starboard bow and exploding as it hit the water. Again the *Inishtrahull* suffered no more harm than a thorough wetting. The Focke-Wulf then made as if to come in for a sixth attack but at the last moment banked steeply to port and flew off in a south-south-westerly direction. It would seem that she had had enough of this stubborn little ship.

Robert Gibson stepped down from his gun with a sigh of relief as he watched the enemy plane dwindle to a tiny speck on the far horizon. There was no doubt in his mind that the Focke-Wulf had fared far worse in the action than his ship. The plane had dropped five bombs, three of which had missed and two had failed to explode. The *Inishtrahull* had been sprayed with bullets and cannon-shells on each bombing run; much of her rigging had been shot away, the wheel-house resembled a colander, and some rails and ladders had been demolished, but she was still a functioning ship. Apart from Gibson himself, whose wounds had been caused by splinters from the shattered wooden wheel-house, there were no casualties. In return, the Focke-Wulf had received a thrashing her crew would remember for a long time. The underside of her fuselage and wings must have been in much the same state as the *Inishtrahull*'s wheel-house, and it was probable that her lower, rear gunner had been either wounded or killed.

There now remained the problem of the unexploded thousand-pound bomb, which still nestled with sinister intent on the collier's foredeck. While having his wounds dressed, Gibson was able to give the matter some thought. His first instinct was to put into Broadhaven, which lay around the next headland, and there call on the Irish Free State authorities to deal with the bomb. But he dismissed this idea quickly. He was suspicious of the so-called neutral Irish, fearing that information would be given to the enemy. Furthermore, he did not wish to delay his ship. He had given his ETA Ayr as daylight on the 14th and had no intention of being late. He would deal with the bomb himself. Leaving Second Mate Hosier in charge of the bridge, Gibson, accompanied by First Mate Dalzell and Chief Engineer Roberts, walked forward to inspect the Focke-Wulf's unwelcome gift.

The bomb lay in the gulley between the forecastle bulkhead and the coaming of the forward hatchway, a fat, grey-painted egg, full of menace and rolling jerkily each time the *Inishtrahull*'s bows rose and fell on the swell. The fins had fallen off, but otherwise the bomb, which contained enough explosive to reduce the collier to a pile of smoking scrap, seemed intact. As it had been dropped from a height of 150 feet without exploding, it seemed reasonable to Gibson – and his senior officers agreed – that the bomb would stand up to some more rough handling. They would deal with it as they habitually dealt with rubbish that cluttered up the *Inishtrahull*'s decks, and that meant dumping it overboard.

When Gibson called his men to the bridge, all thirteen volunteered to tackle the bomb. It was then agreed that Gibson, who was partially incapacitated by his wounds, should take the helm, while Chief Engineer Roberts and one stoker looked after the engines. The rest, with the exception of the cook, who was considered rather too elderly for such strenuous work, collected crowbars, ropes and tackles and made their way purposefully up the foredeck.

Second Engineer Neale Mitchell, a twenty-seven-year-old Belfast man, took charge, first reassuring his party that the bomb was 'probably a bloody dud, anyway'. The laughs turned to worried frowns when it was realized that the derrick with which they had planned to lift the bomb was useless, all its running-gear having been shot away. Five men crouched down by the bomb and tried to lift it, but it would not budge. A rope tackle was then rigged from the derrick boom and a rope strop passed around the body of the bomb, but when the strain was taken on the tackle, it became obvious to Gibson, who was watching from the bridge, that ropes would not take the weight. Not wishing to see the bomb dropped, thereby perhaps wiping out most of his crew, he intervened.

Mitchell conferred with Gibson, and they decided to try a more devious approach. A wire strop was made and passed around the bomb and, using the steam winch and a wire cargo runner led through the head block of the after derrick, the bomb was dragged along the deck until it was just forward of the bridge and under the derrick head. Then the strain was taken on the runner and, with the aid of crowbars, baulks of timber and a great deal of human sweat, the bomb was manhandled onto the hatch-top. Two skids were then laid from the hatch to the ship's-side bulwark and the thousand-pound canister of high explosive was rolled to the ship's side and unceremoniously committed to the deep.

When it was all over, Mitchell and his men found their hands shaking so much that they had difficulty in downing the large tots of rum Captain Gibson saw fit to dispense. For many nights to come, they would relive in their dreams those awesome hours when ten men, straining and cursing, had manhandled half a ton of certain death along the deck and over the side.

The *Inishtrahull* reached the Scottish port of Ayr shortly after daylight on the 14th, less than an hour late on her ETA. She was battered but the loading of her cargo was not long delayed. Three days later, when she arrived back in her home port of Belfast, Robert Gibson and his men found that their story had gone ahead of them, and they received a visit from no less a personage than the Flag Officer in Charge Belfast. The beribboned Rear-Admiral was lavish in his praise for the little company of men who had fought and won against the might of the Luftwaffe.

For his bravery in organizing and leading the operation to dispose of the bomb, Second Engineer Neale Mitchell was awarded the George Medal. Captain Robert Gibson, Second mate Wilfred Hosier and Seamen Gunner William Gregg received a Commendation for their work at the guns. The *Inishtrahull*, having licked her wounds, returned to sea and carried on with her grimy but essential work throughout the rest of the war.

7   The Road to Russia

On 22 June 1812 the armies of Napoleon Bonaparte crossed the borders of Russia, marching towards what was to be one of the most ignominious defeats in military history. One hundred and twenty-nine years later, to the day, Adolf Hitler set out to prove that he could succeed where Bonaparte had failed. On Sunday 22 June 1941, 164 divisions of the German Army, supported by 2,700 aircraft, advanced into the Soviet Union on a front extending from the Baltic to the Black Sea. In the first three months of fighting, the Germans steam-rollered 300 miles deep into Soviet territory.

Although until the time she was attacked the USSR had been openly supporting Germany morally and economically and had turned her back on a Britain fighting alone, her immediate reaction was vociferously to demand all possible help from that country. Despite her own urgent needs at home and in the Middle East, Britain at once offered tanks, aircraft and guns. On 12 August the first convoy carrying war-materials set out from UK ports for North Russia, sailing via Iceland. Thereafter a similar convoy sailed every ten or fourteen days right up until the end of the war.

The dangers facing the ships and men who sailed in the Russian convoys were frightening. Tempestuous seas, fog and blizzard, temperatures down to 40° below zero, round-the-clock daylight in summer and unending darkness in winter all added to the misery of the 2,000-mile passage. At the same time, through every mile steamed, the ships were under constant attack from German U-boats, aircraft and surface units. To sail the Russian convoys was to experience all the rigours of the cruel sea, aggravated by the horrors of war at their most extreme.

In winter, the port of Glasgow, with its twelve straggling miles of dreary quaysides and 400 acres of windswept docks and basins, is not the most desirable resting-place for a ship. In late November 1941, made even more cheerless by the constraints of a war already two years old and by a blanket of cold, persistent drizzle, the Scottish port can have held little charm for the men of the British ship *Harmatris*. That they were soon to face a voyage to Arctic Russia, and all that entailed, perhaps made it just that much more bearable. In fact, there were many aboard the *Harmatris* who would gladly have endured a lifetime of winters in Glasgow rather than sail for Russia.

Built in 1932 at the Lithgow Shipyard, Port Glasgow, just a few miles downstream from her loading-berth, the 5,395-ton *Harmatris* was strongly built on lines of stark practicality and capable of lifting anything from anthracite nuts to railway engines. Her coal-fired steam-engine gave her an operating speed of eight to nine knots, at which she carried her various cargoes with maximum economy. Owned by J. & C. Harrison of London, she was commanded by forty-seven-year-old Captain R.W. Brundle of Hull, who was supported by a crew of forty-six. They included seven DEMS gunners, who manned and maintained her armament of one four-inch, one 20 mm Hispano cannon, five .303 stripped Lewis Machine-guns and two twin .303 Marlins. As an additional defence against attacking aircraft, she also carried two PAC rocket-launchers and five kites.

The *Harmatris* completed loading and sailed from Glasgow on the morning of 27 November, having on board 8,000 tons of military stores, vehicles and ammunition consigned to Archangel on the White Sea. Her instructions were to proceed independently to Reykjavik and there await a convoy to Russia.

The 825-mile passage to Iceland was trouble-free, and the *Harmatris* sailed for Archangel in convoy on 4 December. In view of the ever-present danger of attack by German aircraft and surface ships based in northern Norway, the convoy was routed as far north as the limits of the polar pack-ice would allow. It was expected, therefore, that the passage would take at least ten days. Given that Russian methods of discharging cargo were notoriously slow, Brundle and his men faced the prospect of spending Christmas and New Year in Archangel. This was not something they looked forward to.

Trouble came sooner than anticipated, but not from the enemy. Shortly after leaving Reykjavik, early on 6 December, the convoy ran into a strong south-westerly gale, which increased to storm force as the eye of a depression passed over the ships. The wind then suddenly veered to the north-east, and the sea became very confused and high. The *Harmatris*, having a low centre of gravity due to a concentration of heavy cargo in her lower holds, began to roll violently. Within an hour she had fallen astern of the convoy and was fighting a lonely battle against the angry elements in the grey half-light of the Arctic afternoon. As the day wore on and the ever-lowering clouds turned the twilight into sombre darkness, mountainous seas began to break over the ship, flooding her well-decks and tugging at the tightly wedged tarpaulins of her hatches. Brundle, already deeply concerned for the safety of the vehicles stowed in the tween-decks, was now faced with the possibility of having his hatches stove in. He had no alternative but to ride out the storm hove-to with the wind and sea on the bow. The *Harmatris* would make no progress towards her destination, but the damage to ship and cargo would be kept to a minimum.

At 23.00 Brundle was still on the bridge, but the ship was riding more easily. He was tired, his tongue furred from too many cigarettes and cups of strong coffee, and he longed for a hot bath followed, perhaps, by a few hours sleep. At his side was twenty-three-year-old Third Officer William Watson, officer of the watch. When midnight came, the watch would be taken over by the more experienced Second Officer Young, and then Brundle hoped to be able to go below. This was not to be.

The first hint that all was not well below decks came at 23.30, when it was reported from aft that spray was evaporating into clouds of steam when hitting the deck plates alongside No.4 hatch. Brundle lost no time in ordering the hatch opened for investigation. His worst fears were confirmed when it was found that a lorry stowed in the tween-decks was on fire and had broken adrift. With every lurch of the ship, this blazing torch was slamming into the bales and cases stacked in the sides of the deck, spreading fire and destruction in its wake.

Of all the dangers a seaman has to face in the course of his voyaging, there is none he fears more than fire at sea. For those on shore, a fire is hazard enough but can usually be dealt with relatively easily. A fire on board a ship at sea is another matter. There is no fire brigade to hand to call in; the ship's crew, untrained in the techniques of fire fighting and inadequately equipped, have no alternative but to fight the blaze unaided. Should the fire prove impossible to contain, there is only the last resort of taking to the boats – always assuming the weather is kindly disposed towards such a move. In the case of the *Harmatris*, already fighting for her life against mountainous seas, this means of escape was out of the question. For her crew there would be no running away from the fire.

Nor was time on their side, for in her No.4 lower hold, separated from the fire only by a floor of wooden hatchboards, the *Harmatris* carried ten tons of cordite and a large quantity of small-arms ammunition. Brundle knew that, once the flames penetrated into the lower hold, his ship would be finished. Leaving Third Officer Watson in charge of the bridge, he went aft to assess the situation.

On the after deck Brundle met Chief Officer G. Masterman and Chief Steward R. Peart, who with a team of crew members were rigging hoses preparatory to entering the hatch. As no heavy seas were breaking over the deck, this could be done in comparative safety, but Brundle first instructed Masterman to flood the hold with steam in an attempt to smother the fire.

It is probable that the blaze was now too well established, for the steam had little or no effect, and after a while it became clear they must get the hoses down into the tween-deck. The forward end of the hatch was opened and Chief Officer Masterman, wearing a smoke-helmet and safety line, climbed down into the deck, dragging a fire-hose after him.

The task Masterman had undertaken was a daunting one, for the tween-deck was full of choking black smoke and searing flames. Added to this was the danger presented by the rampaging lorry. The protection afforded by the smoke-helmet (a primitive form of breathing-apparatus fed with outside air by a bellows and hose) was minimal. But with great courage Masterman, a forty-one-year-old West Hartlepool man, turned his hose on the blaze and continued to fight the fire until he was overcome by fumes and smoke. Fortunately the men on deck saw his plight and hauled him out of the hatch before he lost consciousness.

There was no lack of volunteers to take Masterman's place. Chief Steward Peart, a South Wales man in his early twenties, now donned the helmet and spent thirty minutes below fighting the flames before he too was forced to return to the deck. Fearing that an explosion might rip the *Harmatris* open and send her to the bottom, Brundle went forward to the bridge, where he instructed his radio officer to send out a call for help. The SOS was answered by the 1,559-ton British vessel *Zaafaran*, which was acting as rescue ship to the convoy. The *Zaafaran* reported she was proceeding towards the *Harmatris* at her maximum speed of twelve knots. Thus assured that he had secured a chance of survival for his men, Brundle returned aft, and throughout the rest of the night he and Peart spelled each other in the smoke-filled tween-deck in a desperate fight to quell the fire before it reached the explosives in the lower hold.

By 07.30 on the 7th, the battle had been won. The fire was out, the runaway lorry secured, and Brundle was able to radio the *Zaafaran* that her services would not be needed.

Although the ship was no longer in immediate danger, a brief examination of her hatches, where accessible, showed that the terrible battering she had received over the previous twenty-four hours had played havoc with her cargo. In the tween-decks, other vehicles had broken adrift, causing chaos in the cargo around them. It was not possible to gain access to the lower holds but it seemed likely that the damage below would be of the same order. Brundle decided it was pointless to proceed further and radioed the convoy commodore for permission to return to Glasgow to have his cargo examined and restowed. This was approved and the *Harmatris* was brought around onto a southerly course to run for the Clyde with the wind and sea astern.

Far on the other side of the world, where the sun had not yet risen, Japanese carrier-borne aircraft were warming up in preparation for their attack on the American fleet at Pearl Harbor. Before the *Harmatris* reached the safety of the Clyde, the United States would be in the war.

Perhaps the only good to come out of the *Harmatris*'s abortive attempt to reach Russia was that Brundle and his men were able to spend Christmas tied up alongside in Glasgow. This was a small reward for men who had faced so much danger and who by their prompt action and unflinching courage had saved a valuable ship and her cargo from almost certain destruction. But the reward was more than they had asked for and when, on the morning of the 26th, the *Harmatris* was again ready for sea, the tenuous links that had temporarily bound her to the shore were cut without hesitation. There was the business of an unfinished voyage to attend to.

The passage to Iceland in Convoy was accomplished without incident and in weather no worse than was to be expected in the North Atlantic in winter. On New Year's Day 1942 the *Harmatris* once again entered Reykjavik harbour. Seven days later she sailed in Convoy PQ 8, bound for the North Russian port of Murmansk, which lies in the Kola Inlet and near the Finnish border.

Convoy PQ 8 was made up of eight merchant ships escorted by two minesweepers. Once clear of Reykjavik, the merchantmen formed up in two columns of four, with the *Harmatris*, which had been selected as commodore ship, leading one of the columns. For the first two days they experienced strong winds and rough seas, adding to the misery of the sub-zero temperatures and never-ending darkness. Fortunately the elements relented late on the 10th, and the small convoy ran into fine, calm weather. Also, on that night the ocean escort joined, consisting of the cruiser HMS *Trinidad* and the destroyers *Matabele*, *Somali*, *Harrier* and *Speedwell*. This formidible array of strength was a most welcome addition, but the men in the merchant ships knew it also pointed to the many dangers that lay ahead.

The convoy continued on a north-easterly course until, on the 11th, in latitude 73° 45′N, it met with field ice and was forced to divert to the south. Six more days passed quietly, with the ships making eight knots in unbelievably calm weather with maximum visibility. Only the bone-chilling cold and the tedious darkness, relieved by an hour or two of pale daylight each side of noon, marred what might have been a pleasant voyage.

On Saturday 17 November the convoy was deep into the Barents Sea and shaping course for the Kola Inlet. It seemed that the worst dangers had passed, for there was less than sixty miles to go to waters guarded by Soviet forces. At 16.15 the ships were formed into line ahead, with the *Harmatris*, as commodore ship, leading the line. The cruiser *Trinidad* was on her starboard bow, with HMS *Harrier* zigzagging five cables ahead of *Trinidad*. The destroyers *Somali* and *Matabele* were stationed approximately 2,000 yards on the port and starboard beams respectively, while HMS *Speedwell* brought up the rear. Of the local escort, scheduled to join within the next six hours, it had been reported that HMS *Britomart* and HMS *Salamander* were fogbound in the Kola Inlet, where visibility was down to nil. Only HMS *Sharpshooter* had managed to get under way and was proceeding seawards at all possible speed. However, the escort commander, in HMS *Trinidad*, was not unduly worried. No reports had been received of U-boats operating in the area, and the darkness would keep away the enemy bombers. It was his opinion that, at this stage, the only real threat would come from mines. It was unfortunate that the commander had not yet received an Admiralty signal warning of the presence of at least one enemy submarine in the area. Ahead and to starboard of the convoy, *U-454*, commanded by Kapitän-Leutnant Burkhard Hackländer, lay waiting on the surface, hidden in the darkness of the long Arctic night.

At 19.45 Captain Brundle, who had been on the bridge of the *Harmatris* for so long that his feet seemed to have taken root in the deck, rasped the bristles of his chin and decided it was high time he went below for a shave. The weather was clear, and the experienced Chief Officer Masterman had the watch. Brundle walked out into the wing and took a quick look around the horizon. It was empty except for the reassuring silhouettes of the zigzagging escorts. The darkness was too complete to reveal the thin pencil of *U-454*'s periscope breaking the surface on the starboard bow.

Brundle was in the act of drawing aside the curtain at the doorway to his cabin when the torpedo struck the *Harmatris* on her starboard side and exploded with a thunderous roar. Half-deafened, he clawed his way back up to the bridge, where he found that Masterman had already stopped the engines. The chief officer reported that the ship had been hit in No.1 hold, whose hatches and derricks he had seen hurled skywards in the column of water thrown up by the explosion.

First giving the order for the crew to stand by the lifeboats, Brundle went forward with Masterman to assess the damage.

He found the forecastle deck a smoking shambles, and No.1 hatch had lost its tarpaulins and hatches, but there appeared to be no fire down below. The *Harmatris* was noticeably down by the bow, and soundings revealed water in the forward holds, which was rising rapidly. In spite of all this, Brundle decided she would stay afloat for a while yet.

The situation regarding the *Harmatris* was not immediately clear to the escort commander, to whom it was erroneously reported that the merchant ship had been mined. As the depth of water in the area was only ninety fathoms and the commander had still not received the Admiralty's submarine warning, he considered mining a distinct possibility. However, the destroyer *Matabele* then reported having heard torpedo hydrophone effect, and it was decided that suitable precautions must be taken. Accordingly HMS *Matabele* and HMS *Somali* carried out a short but unsuccessful anti-submarine search to seaward of the convoy, where it was thought an attacking U-boat might be. At the same time, HMS *Speedwell* fell back to cover the *Harmatris*.

Aboard the crippled Harrison ship, Brundle and his senior officers were dicussing the possibility of saving the ship when, at 19.35, another explosion occurred on her port side amidships. The *Harmatris* shuddered violently, but there was no flash or column of water peculiar to a torpedo striking, and Brundle concluded that his ship had suffered the additional ignominy of hitting a mine. He too guessed wrongly, for the *Harmatris* had been the recipient of Hackländer's second torpedo.

The damage caused by the second explosion appeared severe, and Brundle, fearing his lifeboats might be smashed in the next attack, decided it was time to get his men off. He signalled *Speedwell* and asked her to close in. The *Harmatris* was abandoned, and all were safely on board the destroyer by 19.45.

Although the *Harmatris* was so far down by the head that her propellor was out of the water, Brundle had ascertained before leaving that her engine-room was still intact. Once on board the destroyer, he discussed with her commander the possibility of taking his ship in tow, so that she might be beached and her cargo saved. After some deliberation, it was agreed that *Speedwell* should attempt to tow the *Harmatris* towards Cape Teriberski, which lay only fifteen miles to starboard. When Brundle called for volunteers to go with him, every member of his crew stepped forward.

Within the hour they were back on board the *Harmatris*, and towing-lines had been passed and made fast. *Speedwell* took the strain, but the damaged merchant ship refused to move. With her funnel pouring black smoke, the destroyer pulled harder but succeeded only in parting the tow wire. On investigation it was found that the first torpedo had caused the *Harmatris*'s starboard anchor to run away and drag on the bottom. The ship had in fact been brought up to her anchor with 130 fathoms of cable out. As the windlass had been shattered by the explosion, there could be no question of raising the anchor. Brundle sent for hammers and punches, and his men set about splitting the cable.

While this work was going on, the convoy, which had scattered after the attack on the *Harmatris*, was being re-formed by the other escorts, the tanker *British Pride* taking over as commodore ship. By 21.30, the seven remaining merchant ships had formed up in line-ahead and resumed their original course at eight knots. This done, HMS *Matebele* was instructed to drop back and assist the *Harmatris*.

At 21.45 HMS *Sharpshooter*, having succeeding in breaking out of the fog-bound Kola Inlet, joined and was stationed on the starboard beam of the convoy. *Matabele*, finding her assistance was not required by the *Harmatris*, rejoined at 22.15 and also took up a position to starboard. Cape Teriberski was now abeam at only ten miles, and at each flash of its powerful light the convoy and its escorts were sharply silhouetted against the night sky. This gave Burkhard Hackländer in *U-454* the chance he had been waiting for. His sights were trained on the tanker *British Pride*, but it was the zigzagging *Matabele* that caught his two torpedoes. The destroyer disappeared in a sheet of flame as her magazine exploded. Only two Ordinary Seamen survived the sinking.

The operation to cut the *Harmatris*'s anchor cable had been proceeding with painful slowness. The fact that the joining shackles had not been split in many a long year, combined with the darkness and the icy cold, was making a difficult job almost impossible. Following the loss of HMS *Matabele*, *Speedwell*'s commander became anxious for the safety of both ships and signalled Brundle that he and his men would be safer aboard the destroyer for the time being. Brundle was loath to leave his ship again but, as the *Harmatris* was now an obvious sitting target, he took the Navy man's advice. A hot meal and a few hours sleep would not go amiss.

Speedwell circled the area throughout the rest of the night, and at 06.00 next morning Brundle took his men back to the *Harmatris*. There they were immediately confronted by a major problem. They discovered that the main steam had been inadvertently left on throughout the night, and the boilers had run dry. This was a catastrophe, for all the deck steam pipes were frozen solid, and all winches were therefore unusable. The task of splitting the cable and bringing aboard towlines was made more difficult but, with a great deal of sweat and colourful language, both were accomplished. At 08.00 on the 18th HMS *Speedwell* commenced towing the *Harmatris* towards Murmansk at five knots. The rest of the convoy had long since disappeared over the horizon, and the two ships were alone.

And still the torment was not yet over for the *Harmatris*. Around noon, in the short twilight that passes as daylight in the Arctic winter, a German aircraft swooped in at mast-top height, spraying the ship with cannon and machine-gun fire. Fortunately the *Harmatris*'s DEMS gunners were already at action stations and returned fire with considerable accuracy. *Speedwell*'s guns joined in, and arcs of tracer from both ships were seen to hit the attacking plane, which then headed for the shore trailing black smoke and losing height. An hour later a second enemy aircraft was sighted, but this one, no doubt aware of the fate of its predecessor, was more cautious. Maintaining a respectable height, it dropped a stick of bombs which fell harmlessly a mile away from the *Harmatris*. The aircraft then flew over the two ships without losing height and fired its guns in a largely futile gesture of aggression. Both *Harmatris* and *Speedwell* replied but no hits were scored on either side.

Ironically, at 14.30 HMS *Speedwell*, having faithfully watched over her disabled charge for nearly twenty hours, suffered her first damage and casualties – but not at the hand of the enemy. A high-pressure steam pipe burst in her boiler-room, and three seamen were badly scalded. Her commander signalled for a Soviet tug, which arrived within the hour and took over the tow. *Speedwell* then headed for Murmansk at full speed to land her injured men. Two additional tugs arrived alongside the

Harmatris at 17.00, and she continued on her slow way, berthing in Murmansk at 08.00 on the 20th.

With his ship safely tied up, Captain Brundle was for the first time able to make a detailed examination of the damage she had sustained. The second torpedo, which had struck amidships on the port side, he found had resulted in remarkably little damage, except for a severe buckling of the hull and deck plates in the area. On the other hand, *U-454*'s first hit had caused chaos. The torpedo had torn a large hole in the hull on the starboard side forward, both the forepeak and the forward watertight bulkheads were fractured and No.1 hold was three-quarters full of water. On deck, the locking-bars of No.1 hatch had been ripped off, and the wooden hatchboards and tarpaulins were missing. The heavy steel hatchbeams lay strewn around the deck, derricks were missing or bent double, and the shrouds and rigging of the foremast were draped with odds and ends of cargo blown out of the hold, giving the mast the appearance of a gigantic Christmas tree. Over all there lay a thick coating of ice and snow, which, in a way, softened the horror of the mauling the ship had received.

Since the *Harmatris* had first set out from Glasgow on that grey November day in 1941, almost two months had passed, two months during which her crew had faced up to and survived more perils than most men will meet in a lifetime. Yet never once did they seriously consider abandoning their appointed task, which was to deliver a desperately needed cargo to the Soviet Union. Whether their valiant efforts were appreciated by the recipients is a matter which will be debated for as long as those who served in the Russian convoys are alive.

The crippling of the *Harmatris* and the sinking of the *Matabele* with such fearful loss of life proved to be the pinnacle of the careers of Burkhard Hackländer and *U-454*. On 1 August 1943 they had the misfortune to be caught on the surface in the Bay of Biscay by a Sunderland of Coastal Command. When the flying-boat dived to attack, *U-454*'s gunners put up such a fierce barrage that the aircraft crashed into the sea, but its bombs had been released at precisely the right moment, and the U-boat was hit and sunk. Hackländer and twelve other survivors of *U-454* were later picked up by the Royal Navy. Thus were the *Harmatris* and *Matabele* avenged.

8   The Voyage of No Return

We are preparing ten ships to sail individually during the
October dark. They are all British ships, for which the
crews will have to volunteer, the dangers being terrible,
and their sole hope if sunk far from help being Arctic
clothing and such heating arrangements as can be placed
in the lifeboats.

Extract from telegram. Winston Churchill to President
Roosevelt 7 October 1942.

In the autumn of 1942, apart from the North Atlantic, where the
U-boats were riding the crest of a bloody wave sending nearly a
hundred merchant ships to the bottom every month, the
momentum of war was beginning to slow. It might even be said
that slowly, very slowly, the tide was turning in the favour of
Britain and her allies.

Although Japanese forces had finally reached the borders of
India, there were signs that they were at the absolute limits of
their long supply lines and would be unable to move further
west. In the Pacific, their swift advance through the islands had
been halted and, as the first move in the long-awaited
counter-attack, American marines had landed on Guadalcanal.
On the Russian Front, the Germans appeared to have fought
themselves to a standstill. The siege of Stalingrad was
crumbling, and it was plain that the Wehrmacht would make no
more progress before the bitter fingers of the Russian winter
closed around it. In the Mediterranean, the situation, although
still precarious, was even more hopeful. Montgomery had taken
over in the Western Desert in August and had already stopped
Rommel dead in his tracks. Preparations were now well in hand

for a counter-attack designed to push the Germans back along the road to Tripoli. Coincident with this, it was planned that British and American forces would invade Morocco and Algeria in force from the sea.

Such momentous events meant little to the people of downtown Philadelphia as they stirred sluggishly to the rising sun on a morning in early October that year. In comparison with that other world across the Atlantic Ocean, where the cut and thrust of war were an exciting reality, life in Philadelphia was normal to the point of boredom. The excitement of Pearl Harbor had long since faded into history, the necessities of life were in abundance, there were no air raids, no threat of invasion, nothing in fact to quicken the pulses of those who had seen the coming of war as a great Hollywood adventure.

Down on the waterfront, where the morning mist still swirled over the Delaware, the mood was in sharp contrast. The wharves from Market Street to Greenwich Point were jammed with ocean-going ships, American and British, all painted overall in wartime grey. Even at this early hour, steam winches clattered and derrick blocks squealed as ton after ton of military equipment was whisked up off the dusty quays and lowered into the holds of the waiting ships. Philadelphia's longshoremen were caught up in 'Operation Torch', the projected Allied invasion of North Africa.

Only one ship lay idle at the wharves, her hatches battened down and her derricks lowered to rest. She was the British ship *Chumleigh*, already loaded to her hatch-tops with 5,000 tons of army stores and due to sail before the sun set over the frowning Appalachians.

The 5,445-ton *Chumleigh*, registered in London, was owned by the Cardiff-based Tatem Steam Navigation Company and had been built in 1938 by William Pickersgill of Sunderland. In outward appearance she was a typical South Wales tramp, But inwardly she differed radically from most of her miserable contemporaries. William James Tatem, Baron Glanely of St Fagans, being a self-made man, had had a penchant for the good things of life which had spilled over into the superior accommodation of his ships. The *Chumleigh*'s cabins, for both officers and crew, were spacious and well furnished, her elegant dining-saloon was panelled in polished mahogany, and her captain's quarters would not have disgraced a first-class hotel.

The *Chumleigh* carried a total crew of fifty-eight, many of whom had already endured three years of war at sea, much of that period spent in the North Atlantic, where there was little respite from the marauding U-boats and Focke-Wulfs. It would not then be surprising to find that, to a man, they welcomed the prospect of a voyage to the Mediterranean, where the sun shone and the torpedoes and bullets were less abundant. As yet, the *Chumleigh* had been given no destination for her cargo, but it was obvious to all on board that she was to be part of the invasion fleet. It was assumed she would be told to leave her berth during the day to anchor in Chesapeake Bay to await a convoy.

Chief Officer Ernest Fenn, having worked late into the previous night preparing the *Chumleigh*'s cargo papers, was on deck early with Boatswain Andrew Hardy checking on the ship's readiness for sea. No seaman worth his mettle will venture out into the Atlantic unprepared for bad weather, and forty-five-year-old Fenn, well versed in the ways of the sea, was no exception. With Hardy at his side, he checked and double-checked hatch tarpaulins, derricks, ventilators, air pipes, anything on deck the sea could make mischief with. The equinoctial gales were abroad in the Atlantic, and the *Chumleigh* might well be shipping green seas within hours of clearing Cape Henlopen.

On the *Chumleigh*'s bridge, Second Officer James Starkey and Third Officer David Clark were likewise engaged in preparing for the forthcoming voyage. Starkey was in the chart-room making last-minute corrections to the Mediterranean charts, while Clark haunted the wheel-house, running a critical eye over the code flags and signalling-equipment.

Below decks, in the engine-room, forty-seven-year-old Chief Engineer Richard Colvin was on his rounds, accompanied by his second engineer, Richard Middlemiss. In deference to the start of a new voyage, both men wore clean white boilersuits as they ran critical hands and eyes over the gleaming engine and its auxiliaries, an occasional nod of satisfaction being their only communication. The *Chumleigh*'s triple expansion steam-engine, built by Richardsons, Westgarth & Company of

Hartlepool, would set no speed records, but it was as solid and reliable as the men who looked after it.

Breakfast-time came around, and with it the inevitable arrival of the ship's chandler and a late delivery of fresh stores. Chief Steward Islwyn Davies cursed the clause in Sod's Law that decrees that the arrival of stores always coincides with the serving of a meal. Followed by his stewards and cooks, he marched purposefully down the gangway to tackle the small mountain of sacks of potatoes and carrots, nets of cabbages, boxes of eggs and cases of fruit, all to be brought aboard and stowed in their respective lockers.

In his cabin below the bridge, Captain Daniel Morley Williams caught the smell of frying bacon drifting up from the galley, checked his watch and reached for his uniform jacket. He was leaving the cabin for the dining-saloon when he received an official and most unwelcome visitor.

The tight-lipped official brought orders from the Admiralty for the *Chumleigh* to sail at once, to proceed at all speed to Halifax, Nova Scotia, and there to join a convoy bound eastwards across the North Atlantic. Williams ate his bacon, cold and greasy, between two pieces of bread, while the tugs plucked the *Chumleigh* off her berth and pointed her bows down river.

Daniel Williams was on his first voyage in comand, having previously served in the *Chumleigh* as chief officer. The promotion had come out of the blue when, in July that year, the ship had returned to London after a particularly harrowing trip to Russia. The ageing Captain Priestly, weary of the knocks of war, had decided to retire on arrival, and Williams had found himself moving his belongings into the master's cabin.

Those summer days spent in Surrey Commercial Docks while London basked in the sunshine, for the time being free of air raids, had been heady ones indeed for Williams. His nerves were still raw from the horrors of the Archangel run, and he found blessed relief in the new responsibilities suddenly heaped on his shoulders.

At thirty-five, Daniel Williams was tall and lean, with a keen sense of humour and dark, curly hair betraying his Celtic origins. Born in the quiet Cardiganshire village of Llangranog, son of a farmer, he was a first-class seaman and navigator. He was also a natural leader, a man who had the rare ability to be strict but scrupulously fair and to be kind without being indulgent. Long before the *Chumleigh* reached Philadelphia, Williams had earned the respect and loyalty of his crew.

When the *Chumleigh* entered the outer harbour of Halifax, Nova Scotia, the grey waters of the bay were covered with ships as far as the eye could see. More than forty British and Allied ships were assembled at anchor, awaiting the word to sail westwards. The word was not long in coming. Only a few hours after the *Chumleigh*'s arrival, the convoy was under way and heading out into the Atlantic. For most of the ships, this was to be just another routine passage, a 2,400-mile slog across an ocean bedevilled by storms and infested with U-boats. For the crews of the British merchantmen in particular, who had been through it so many times before, it was a case of biting the bullet and concentrating thoughts on the welcome waiting on the other side – assuming they reached it. Williams, who had been hustled ashore in Halifax for a briefing by the Naval Control, had the unpleasant task of telling his own crew that, for them, it would be different. The *Chumleigh* was going back to Russia.

In the spring of 1942, when Hitler came to realize that the conquest of the Soviet Union would not be the easy campaign he had envisaged, he turned his attention to those who were supplying the Soviets with arms and equipment. At that time Allied convoys were going through to Murmansk and Archangel at the rate of two a month. Heavy units of the German Navy, including the *Tirpitz*, the *Hipper* and the *Admiral Scheer*, were already operating against these convoys from the Norwegian fjords, but with little success. It was decided to send more U-boats and bombers north to rectify the situation. At that time of the year, the convoys were sailing in almost continuous daylight and were particularly vulnerable. The losses began to mount and culminated in June in the slaughter of Convoy PQ 17, which lost twenty-four ships out of thirty-five. Over 130,000 tons of vital war supplies went to the bottom, and hundreds of Allied merchant seamen died horribly in the icy waters beyond the Arctic Circle.

Following the débâcle of PQ 17, despite insistent Soviet cries for ever more cargoes, it was decided to suspend all deliveries until the Arctic winter brought the cover of darkness twenty-four hours a day. Even then, the wisdom of sending large, heavily escorted convoys was questioned. As an experiment, it was thought best first to send through ten ships sailing independently and unescorted. The *Chumleigh* was to be one of the chosen ten.

The passage across the North Atlantic was arduous but uneventful. Seven days out from Halifax, the *Chumleigh* broke off from the convoy and headed north-east for Iceland. An hour later she was alone, with only the long, heaving swells in sight as far as the eye could see. Williams was well aware of the dangers of being abroad in the Atlantic without the shield of the Royal Navy, and as the *Chumleigh* made her lonely way to the north-east, look-outs were doubled and guns manned around the clock.

For a supposedly non-combatant merchant ship, the *Chumleigh* was well armed. She mounted, in addition to the customary four-inch gun on her poop, a quick-firing Bofors, four 20 mm Oerlikons, two Marlin machine-guns and the usual array of PAC and FAM rockets for defence against low-flying aircraft. The guns were manned and maintained by a force of eighteeen DEMS gunners, nine of whom were seconded from the Royal Navy and nine from the Maritime Anti-Aircraft Regiment. In the event of an attack coming from the surface of the sea or from the air, the *Chumleigh* was capable of a credible defence. Against underwater attack she was, like all merchant ships, completely defenceless.

As luck would have it, the *Chumleigh* was not called upon to use her guns, and she arrived at the Icelandic port of Hvalfjord on time and unharmed. A few days later, at 17.00 on 31 October, in company with nine other ships, four British and five American, she sailed out into the uninviting darkness of a bitterly cold night. Once outside the harbour, the ships split up to go their own several ways. Operation 'FB' had begun.

After rounding the north of Iceland, Williams was instructed to make first for a position 250 miles north of Jan Mayen Island, thence to pass thirty miles south of Spitzbergen and then in a south-easterly direction towards the White Sea and Archangel. The total distance was no more than 2,500 miles, but it was a passage that would take the *Chumleigh* through some of the most inhospitable waters in the world. The strain of sailing in constant darkness would be aggravated by dense fog, blinding snowstorms and temperatures falling to as much as 80° below freezing. To all this was added the threat of a powerful and unseen enemy lying in wait along the way.

For Daniel Williams, as yet only a few months in command, the passage promised to be the ultimate test of his ability and courage. The *Chumleigh*, in common with many British merchant ships of her day, was equipped with only the minimum requirements in navigational aids. Her owner's generosity, revealed in her elegant accommodation, had stopped short at the bridge, where the old rule of 'lead, log and look-out' still prevailed. Her only 'modern' aid to navigation was a wireless-telegraph (W/T) direction-finder, an instrument which would be of little use to her on the passage to Archangel, as there were no shore radio-beacons operating that far north. With the prospect of continually overcast skies and poor visibility, she would have to rely almost exclusively on dead reckoning. At the Admiralty briefing prior to sailing from Hvalfjord, Williams had drawn attention to this, but the Senior Naval Officer could only offer sympathy. He pointed out that the supplies they were carrying to Russia were so urgently needed that all risks were justifiable. He urged the ships to press on at all possible speed, for ice was already forming in the approaches to Archangel.

It was as Williams had feared. Rounding the north point of Iceland, the *Chumleigh* ran into heavily overcast skies, with hazy visibility and frequent blinding snowstorms. Accurate navigation was out of the question. As far as could be ascertained, the position off Jan Mayen was reached in the early hours of 3 November, and course was then altered to pass thirty miles clear of the southern point of Spitzbergen. There had been no improvement in the weather, and by that time Williams was becoming concerned at the accuracy of his magnetic compasses, which were unpredictable in those high latitudes. When a momentary break in the clouds later that day enabled a quick azimuth to be taken of a bright star, both compasses were found to be eight degrees in error.

Late that night, the *Chumleigh*'s wireless operator listened in to a series of distress messages. Some 350 miles to the south, several of the other vessels taking part in Operation 'FB' were under attack by German long-range bombers operating from bases in the north of Norway. For the first time, Williams began to bless the protective mantle of fog and driving snow through which his ship was sailing.

At 01.00 on the 5th, a radio message was received from Admiralty instructing the *Chumleigh* to steer north to latitude 77 degrees before shaping her course to pass south of Spitzbergen. In view of attacks on the other ships to the south, two of which had been sunk, it had been decided to keep the *Chumleigh* well out of harm's way. That was all very well, but Williams had had no further opportunity to check his compasses since the morning of the 3rd. Another alteration of course would only serve to make the ship's position even more doubtful. In the hope that the cloud might break, he postponed altering to the north until 05.00. This was a decision he was to regret, for at 11.00, during the brief period of twilight, a German reconnaissance seaplane dived out of the overcast sky and began to circle the ship, taking care to keep out of range of her guns.

The aircraft made no move to attack and soon flew off, but Williams knew that the position of his vessel was already being reported to the bomber bases, some 400 miles to the south. The JU-88s would not be long in coming. An hour later, when the DR plot showed the *Chumleigh* to be in approximately 77 degrees North, course was altered to the south to return to the original route.

Throughout the remainder of that day, the atmosphere on board was tense as the *Chumleigh* steamed southwards with the threat of air attack hanging over her. Daniel Williams paced the bridge feeling that his thirty-five years had in the space of a few days been doubled. The bombs and torpedoes of the enemy he had come to live with in his three years of war at sea, but the nagging uncertainty of not knowing exactly where his ship was in relation to the land weighed heavily on his mind. For too long he had been steaming blind, altering course on positions based on no more than an educated guess. He was unsure of his ship's speed and without any means of checking the deviation on his compasses. This was an extremely dangerous situation, and he feared the outcome.

By evening, great white flakes of snow had begun to fall, seriously reducing the visibility. There was a freshening breeze from the south, and a moderate swell was running. At 23.00 Williams checked his calculations on the chart for the last time and, having established to the best of his ability that the ship was clear of the southern point of Spitzbergen, gave the order to alter course to the east. He then walked out into the wing of the bridge and stood peering into the driving snow, wondering if he had made the right decision.

Half an hour later the *Chumleigh* ran headlong onto a reef off Spitzbergen's South Cape. She was twenty miles to the north of her intended course.

When the initial shock of the sudden grounding had faded, it became apparent that the *Chumleigh* had ridden up over the reef and was firmly held amidships. Her bow sloped down so that the foredeck was awash, and her stern was almost out of the water. Thus balanced, Williams feared she would soon break her back.

But the *Chumleigh*, built in one of the finest shipyards on Britain's north-east coast, was made of sterner stuff. She was still intact nearly two hours later, and Williams decided there might still be a chance of saving her. But first he deemed it prudent to put most of his crew into the lifeboats, to lay off the ship in case she broke up and sank without warning. He would stay on board with Chief Officer Ernest Fenn and Second Engineer Middlemiss, a thirty-seven-year-old Scot from Edinburgh.

After the long ordeal the men of the *Chumleigh* had been through, culminating in the grounding of their ship on an unseen reef in a cold and inhospitable sea, it can be appreciated that their morale was now at a low ebb. It was not surprising, therefore, that when Williams gave the order to take to the boats, a certain amount of panic set in. By the time Third Officer David Clark made his way down from the bridge to take charge of his lifeboat, he found that his crew had already started to lower away. In the darkness, the after fall was accidentally cast off and the boat plummeted to the water stern first, throwing out the two men aboard at the time. The boat was swamped and the two unfortunate men disappeared in the icy water. Clark, a twenty-two-year-old soft-spoken Devon man, calmed his men and distributed them amongst the other boats.

In spite of the big swell running, the three remaining lifeboats were launched smoothly and taken away from the ship's side.

Meanwhile Williams, Fenn and Middlemiss remained on the bridge, Williams being occupied with dumping overboard all confidential papers and books in their weighted bags.

Having discharged his last duty to the Admiralty, Williams was returning to the wheelhouse when he heard a faint cry for help coming from below. He ran down to the main deck and, shining his torch overside, saw two men struggling in the water. They were the two unfortunates who had been thrown out of the Third Officer's boat when it up-ended. Realizing that the men could not last much longer in the icy water, Williams called to one of the boats, which had drifted back alongside, to go to their rescue. Unfortunately the boat's crew, possibly still numb with shock at their predicament, made no move to carry out his orders. Daniel Williams, normally slow to anger, saw red, clambered down into the boat and physically forced its crew into action. With the help of Boatswain Hardy and one of the *Chumleigh*'s young apprentices, he hauled one of the drowning men out of the water and into the boat. The man was rigid with cold and very near to death but he revived when brandy was poured down his throat. The other man was not so fortunate. By the time the boat reached him, he was dead.

Williams now returned on board the *Chumleigh*, but so exhausted was he by his exertions that he collapsed on reaching the deck. However, he quickly recovered and was soon discussing with Fenn and Middlemiss the possibility of refloating the ship. At 02.30 the lifeboats were called back alongside, and Williams asked for volunteers to assist with the operation. It was also in his mind that his men would be safer, and certainly warmer, back on board the ship. but the men in the boats were of a different mind. It was only after some persuasion that two firemen agreed to reboard to help Second Engineer Middlemiss raise steam.

As soon as the engines were ready, Williams made an attempt to back the ship clear of the reef, but after running full astern for half an hour, he was forced to admit defeat. In fact, his efforts resulted only in settling the ship more firmly on the reef. Her bow and stern were now sagging dangerously and, fearful she was about to break her back, Williams rang 'finished with engines' and called Middlemiss and his men on deck. There was nothing more to be done to save the ship.

In what he knew to be a largely futile gesture, but one that for the sake of protocol he must make, Williams now brought one of his radio officers back on board to send a message informing all stations that the *Chumleigh* was being abandoned. At 04.00, 4½ hours after striking the reef, Williams took a last sad look around the deserted deck of his ship, swung his leg over the bulwarks and climbed down into the waiting lifeboat.

As the boats pulled away from the *Chumleigh*, the driving snow began to ease, and it was only then that Williams was able to see the awful danger into which he had unwittingly steamed his ship. She was trapped in a horseshoe-shaped lagoon with angry breakers on all sides. There seemed to be no escape. He wisely decided to put the boats back alongside the ship until the short Arctic twilight gave him the opportunity to assess the situation carefully.

Five or six hours later, when there was sufficient light, an opening was sighted in the reefs, and the three lifeboats once again left the shelter of the *Chumleigh*'s hull and pulled for the open sea. They were not a moment too soon. Low down on the horizon, five aircraft were seen heading in towards the ship. As they drew nearer, Williams recognized them as JU-88 heavy bombers, which were no doubt responding to the call of the seaplane which had haunted them briefly some twenty-four hours previously.

The aircraft began to circle the lifeboats ominously, and for a time the survivors, who had already been through so much, thought they were about to be machine-gunned for good measure. But the planes sheered off and directed their attack on the stranded *Chumleigh*. A number of bombs were dropped on the captive target from mast-top height, at least two of which scored direct hits. When the aircraft flew away, a column of black smoke was seen to be rising from the ship.

Having been forced to watch his ship suffer this further indignity, Daniel Williams, tired and miserable though he was, now set his mind to the problem of survival. Although the southern coast of Spitzbergen was in sight, he knew it was pointless to make for it. The Admiralty pilot book described it as a land of sheer ice cliffs and wandering glaciers, completely devoid of vegetation and uninhabited except for polar bears and Arctic foxes. To put the boats ashore there – if that were indeed possible – would only add to their problems. The nearest inhabitation lay 150 miles to the north, at the Soviet mining settlement of Barentsburg, and it was for there that they must make. He gave the order to set sail.

The weather had now improved, and at first good progress was made. However, the smaller of the three boats soon began to drop astern, and Williams decided it would be better to abandon it and redistribute its crew amongst the two larger boats. When this was done, they set off again, hugging the coast and sailing smartly before a fresh breeze. Williams's boat, with Third Officer Clark at the helm, had on board a total of twenty-eight, while Fenn's boat carried twenty-nine. Both boats were overcrowded but, in the bitterly cold conditions prevailing, this proved to be an advantage.

During the night the two boats became separated, but Williams continued on his course, confident that Fenn would join up with him later. But on the morning of the 7th their luck began to run out when the wind fell away and they were becalmed for most of the day. The situation changed dramatically for the worse on the 8th, which brought with it a full gale and a short, heavy sea. The crowded boat was in danger of being swamped, and Williams was forced to stream the sea anchor and heave to. Throughout that day and the following night, they drifted, with the waves from time to time breaking right over the boat. They were cold, wet and thoroughly demoralized. It was only the indomitable Daniel Williams who, by bullying his men into bailing their waterlogged boat, kept them alive.

On the morning of the 9th, the weather eased, but they found they had drifted out of sight of the land. The boat was equipped with a small engine, for which there was a limited supply of fuel. This Williams had been saving for such an emergency as now faced them – for if they lost touch with the land completely, they were finished. The engine was started and they steered back toward the east. After running under power for about two hours, it was with great relief that they sighted not only the coast but the other lifeboat. The two boats came together, and Williams and Fenn were able to confer. They calculated they were no more than eighty miles south of Barentsburg, and it was mutually agreed that Williams should push on ahead, using his engine to reach port and bring help for the others. This providential meeting between the two boats acted on their crews like a tonic, and when the boats parted company again, the men were in high spirits.

Using both engine and sail, Williams estimated that his boat would reach Barentsburg in fourteen or fifteen hours – a gruelling passage but survivable. But their recent good fortune was short-lived. During the night, the wind rose and the temperature plummeted. The boat began to ship water, and soon the bottom boards were awash. A thick layer of ice formed on the gunwales, and the sails became frozen boards. Fortunately the water in the bottom of the boat did not freeze, and the men were able to keep it at a reasonable level by bailing. But later, to add to their misery, their clothes froze to their bodies. It seemed they were condemned to die where they sat, with their feet in icy water, their bodies buffeted by a cruel wind, and the relentless cold eating into their bones. Only the sheer force of William's personality stopped them giving up there and then.

The first to slip away was the chief steward, Islwyn Davies. In the small, lonely hours of the 19th, thirty-year-old Davies, despite the best efforts of his companions, fell into a delirium and died as quietly as he had lived. As he committed the body of his fellow Welshman to the deep, Daniel Williams cursed the cruelty of a war that had brought this man all the way from the gentle hills of his native Ceredigion to die in the desolate wastes of the Barents Sea.

Pushing on through the rest of the night, under sail only in order to conserve his dwindling supply of fuel, Williams restarted the engine at the first hint of light. He calculated that they must now be very close to Icefjord, the large ice-free fjord at whose mouth lay Barentsburg. A few hours later, in the last of the twilight, Prince Charles Foreland, at the entrance to the fjord, was sighted, and with mounting hope Williams altered towards the headland. At that moment the boat's engine spluttered and died. All attempts to restart it were unsuccessful.

The morale of the men in the boat now tumbled to a new low. They were all desperately weak and, although it was not then apparent to them, suffering from frostbite in varying degrees. Huddled together for warmth, they had lost the will to eat and were experiencing excruciating pangs of thirst which the lifeboat's meagre supply of fresh water could not assuage. At least one man, the ship's donkeyman, was delirious. The most grievous blow of all fell when Captain Williams, worn out by five days of constant mental and physical strain, lapsed into unconsciousness. Robbed of their gallant leader, it seemed that there was now no hope for any of them.

In the blackness of the freezing night, alone on the heaving ocean, the tiny boat became an island of despair. This might well have been the point at which the story ended but, as in all walks of life, when one leader falls, another rises to take his place. In this case it was twenty-two-year-old Third Officer David Clark.

The ink was barely dry on Clark's second mate's certificate, but what he lacked in experience he made up for in determination. Although his hands and feet were so frostbitten that he had no feeling in either, he immediately took command of the lifeboat when Williams lost consciousness.

The task facing Clark would have daunted many men twice his age. In his hands was a partially waterlogged boat containing twenty-seven men, two of whom, including Williams, seemed to be dying. The others were cold, wet, thirsty and without hope. The boat's engine had failed and they were drifting within sight of an unknown shore. Clark decided to wait until there was some light in the sky before committing himself to a course of action.

When the sky lightened, shortly before noon on the 11th, the land was no longer in sight. Clark drove his men to hoist the sails, which proved a great effort, as the canvas was frozen hard and they were all very weak. An hour later, the land was again visible, and Clark began to search for a landing-place. He had hoped to be able to make Barentsburg, but as the cold was so severe and his men so exhausted, he realized that, unless they reached the shore and found shelter quickly, they would all die.

As they slowly closed the land, breakers were sighted and it soon became evident that a line of reefs ran parallel to the coast as far as the eye could see. The disappointment of those in the boat was great and soon to be compounded by a gale-force wind and rough seas which broke over the gunwales. Clark altered course to the south and began to sail along outside the reef. He had no idea of his position but knew he must find a way through the reef. He must put an end to this awful nightmare.

Soon after complete darkness had again closed in, flickering lights were seen on shore. This sign that they were not after all alone in this dark, frozen world raised a cheer from half a dozen pairs of cracked lips. Clark was quick to take advantage of the temporary upsurge in morale and decided to tackle the reef. The sails were dropped, oars shipped, and they altered boldly towards the shore.

A number of times during the next few hours Clark thought he had found a break in the reef, but each time he was forced to pull back when the opening proved to be no more than an illusion, a momentary slackening in the surge of the sea. Then, just before 02.00 on the morning of the 12th, when Clark was on the point of giving up and heading back out to sea, the gods took pity on them. A huge ground swell picked up the heavily laden boat, carried it across the reef and threw it onto the beach. Bruised, battered, cold and wet, the survivors of the *Chumleigh* had landed.

Half in and half out of the grounded lifeboat. Clark disentangled himself from the jumble of bodies and crawled a few yards up the shingle beach on his hands and knees. When he got unsteadily to his feet, he found it hard to believe the sight that met his eyes. Twenty yards further up on the beach stood a group of wooden huts. If Clark had had the strength to cheer, he would have done so then.

But the night of suffering was not yet over. Many of the survivors were so weak that to crawl the twenty yards to safety was beyond them. For three of the small company, the shock of the heavy landing on the beach had been too much. They died where they lay, gasping out their last breaths on a cold, alien shore.

It took the remainder of the night for Clark and the few others who were capable to drag, carry and cajole the rest up the short stretch of beach and into the shelter of the huts. Captain Williams had by that time regained consciousness but he was very weak.

The huts, as Clark had anticipated, were peopled only by the ghosts of whalers of another age, but they were at least shelter from the biting wind. Without bothering to strip off their sodden clothing, the survivors lay down and were asleep within minutes.

Next morning, as soon as it was light enough to investigate further, one hut was found to contain a small wood-burning stove, matches and a supply of tinned food, including coffee beans. All twenty-three men, refreshed by their night's sleep, moved into that hut and set about making themselves comfortable. The stove was lit, and when it was roaring, snow was melted to make coffee. The hot drink, the first they had tasted for eight days, breathed new life into them, and they began to look to the future. The more active members of the party, led by Clark, rummaged the other huts and returned in triumph with tins of biscuits and corned beef. When the remaining lifeboat rations were added to the store, and it was discovered there was no shortage of driftwood to burn in the stove, life took on a new perspective.

After a few days in the warmth of the hut, Captain Williams recovered sufficiently to take command of the party again. Most of his men, he found, were in a very poor physical condition, having frostbite in their hands and dreadfully swollen feet. They were suffering from 'immersion foot', a painful and dangerous inflamation caused by the long immersion of their feet in the icy water at the bottom of the lifeboat. David Clark, whose superhuman efforts had sustained them and brought them to land while Williams lay unconscious, was particularly badly affected. Only the four Army gunners in the party seemed to be in a reasonable physical shape. One of them, twenty-year-old Gunner Reginald Whiteside, four feet eleven in his boots and an ex-Liverpool docker, showed no more effects of the long ordeal than if he had been on a routine training exercise. Whiteside's toughness and cheery manner were to be an inspiration to all in the days to come.

But again it was Daniel William's determined and effective leadership and exercise of discipline under the most difficult circumstances that were to hold the men together. From the outset, he created and fostered the belief that it would only be a matter of days before rescue arrived. It was just as well he was not aware that the SOS sent out before abandoning the *Chumleigh* had been received by no one, except, perhaps, the hostile ears of the German bomber base in Norway. He was also not to know that the lifeboat containing Ernest Fenn and twenty-eight others had disappeared from the face of the sea, never to be seen again. As far as the outside world was concerned, the *Chumleigh* was missing, believed sunk with all hands, and no rescue operation would be mounted. Williams and his men were alone in a land of ice and snow, a land where no tree or bush grew and where only the glowering, frozen mountains looked down on them in the short half-light of the Arctic day.

Inevitably, although the men now had warmth and a supply of food, the grievous hardships they had suffered began to take their toll. In the first four days, thirteen died from gangrene, brought on by frostbite and immersion foot. With no medical supplies to hand, Williams could do nothing for them, other than comfort them and see to their burial when they were gone. In this he was assisted by his only fit men, the Army gunners, led by twenty-three-year-old Lance Sergeant Richard Peyer. In addition to nursing the sick, the gunners took over the running of the camp, foraging for food and fuel in the time-honoured tradition of the British Army.

The first organized attempts to reach civilization were made by Third Officer Clark and Lance-Sergeant Peyer, who twice set off in the direction in which it was thought Barentsburg lay. Without skis or proper protective clothing, their attempts were doomed from the start, for the ground they had to cover resembled a moonscape, with jagged rocks underfoot, deep ravines and vast, empty areas of snow and ice. Twice Clark and Peyer set out and twice they came back, beaten by the cruel terrain.

As November slipped into December, winter came in earnest, with increased cold and blizzards reducing visibility to a few yards. The short twilight they had so looked forward to in breaking the awful monotony of the almost total darkness shrank to a momentary greying of the sky around noon, and the men's spirits sank proportionately. The diet of biscuits and corned beef, supplemented by Horlicks tablets from the lifeboat, was enough for subsistence but dull and unappetizing. As is often the case under such circumstances, the survivors spent many hours discussing food, savouring over again meals they had eaten in the past and planning the sumptuous banquets they would indulge in when they again reached civilization. However, imagination is a poor substitute for protein, and although their gastric juices flowed, they grew steadily weaker.

Williams was acutely conscious that lack of hope would kill them quicker than lack of sustenance and fought all the time to keep the flame of confidence alive. He persuaded those who were fit enough to take at least two hours exercise a day and, so far as the visibility would allow, encouraged exploration in the vicinity of the camp. When a disused lighthouse was discovered on a nearby cape, hopes rocketed: here perhaps was a chance to signal for help. Unfortunately all the essential parts of the light had been removed, and their elation was short-lived.

In the first week of December Lance-Sergeant Peyer, Gunner Whiteside and Gunner James Burnett volunteered to make another sortie in search of help. Setting off up the fjord in a north-easterly direction, they marched for several hours across the frozen, rocky wilderness before they were forced to turn back. But their attempt did not go unrewarded. On the return journey they came upon a small, isolated hut which contained a sack of flour and some tins of corned beef and cocoa. These they carried back in triumph to the camp.

This latest find came at an opportune time, for the lifeboat rations and original stock of food were running out. For the next month the survivors lived on small cakes made of flour and water. It was a far cry from *haute cuisine*, but with hot drinks – a choice of coffee or cocoa served three times a day – life was bearable for a while. When the coffee and cocoa ran out, they drank hot water. When the flour had gone the same way, they ate whale blubber, a few tins of which they had found in their foraging.

In mid-December Williams, who was beginning to find strength in desperation, set out with Whiteside to make yet another strike in the direction of Barentsburg. As before, they were beaten by the elements and terrain and forced to return to camp without a message of hope. No more food was found and the survivors were reduced to drinking the boiled oil in which the whale blubber had been stored. Even for men who were close to starving, this rank, glutinous mess proved nauseous.

As Christmas drew near, with nothing but the ever-present snow to remind them of a season they once knew as festive, the situation in the hut grew worse day by day. Clark and the boatswain, Hardy, were in a very weak condition, suffering from gangrene in their hands and feet. Several others also had gangrenous limbs, which oozed pus. The stench in the small hut was unbearable.

Christmas Eve saw the death of another man, and Williams then decided he must make a final effort to get help or – and he knew this was a distinct possibility – die in the attempt. He took with him Peyer and Whiteside and set out up the fjord, forcing the pace as much as he dared. When they had covered what Williams estimated to be about half the distance to Barentsburg, the tough little ex-docker, Whiteside, at last broke down and could go no further; Peyer was also near to collapse, so Williams had no alternative but to turn back.

The first day of 1943 was welcomed in an air of abject misery. There was no more food left, and the nine remaining men were sustained only by melted snow water and the warmth of the stove, in which they were now burning planks torn from the other huts. On the morning of 2 January Whiteside – one of the few men still able to move – went outside to bring more fuel for the stove. A few minutes later he threw open the door of the hut, his eyes wide, his speech incoherent.

Believing the gunner had gone mad, Williams struggled to his feet and tried to calm him. But he could make no sense of the man's hysterical raving. It then occurred to him that the hut was about to be attacked by bears, for several had been seen in the vicinity of the camp. Cautiously he went outside and there he saw two white-suited figures skiing towards the hut. As suddenly as it had begun on that dark, storm-filled night off the South Cape fifty-eight days before, the nightmare was over.

The newcomers, two Norwegian soldiers on a routine patrol from Barentsburg, were appalled by the sight that met them in the hut. The nine survivors, gaunt, hollow-eyed, their clothes in rags and with evil-smelling pus soaking through the makeshift bandages on their hands and feet, simply stared back in disbelief.

Quickly sizing up the situation, the Norwegians handed over all the food and cigarettes they had in their rucksacks and immediately set off to return to Barentsburg to bring help. With them went Gunners Whiteside and Burnett, determined to reach the outside world on their own two feet and with their heads held high. The indomitable Reginald Whiteside did just that, but James Burnett, who had used up his last reserves of strength, had to submit to being half-carried in the final stages of the journey.

Early next day, two sledge parties arrived at the hut, bringing with them food, clothing and a doctor. Clark and Hardy, by then seriously ill, were taken back to Barentsburg at once. The doctor and two men stayed with Williams and the four other survivors until more men and sledges arrived next day. At 20.00 they reached the goal which had eluded them for fifty-three days. It was no comfort for them to learn that, all through those long, anguished days and nights of suffering. Barentsburg had lain only twelve miles away.

All nine survivors were hospitalized in Barentsburg, where they were nursed back to health, a process which took over two months. Another two months were to pass before the cruisers HMS *Bermuda* and HMS *Cumberland* arrived in Icefjord, and Daniel Williams and the only eight men of his crew to survive the sinking of the *Chumleigh* were returned to Britain. They landed in Thurso in northern Scotland on 15 June 1943, more than seven months after the loss of their ship. For six of those months they had been officially reported as missing, believed lost at sea.

For his outstanding courage and leadership, Daniel Morley Williams was awarded the OBE. Richard Peyer, Reginald Whiteside and James Burnett received the BEM.

Sadly, the *Chumleigh* had not been allowed to rest in peace while her men were fighting for their lives. Eleven days after she ran aground, she was torpedoed by *U-625* and again bombed by JU-88s. Her rusting bones still lie off the southern point of Spitzbergen, a grim monument to the fifty-one members of her crew who died in a vain attempt to bring help to the Soviet Union.

9   All Roads Lead to St Paul's

The British ship *Teesbank* cleared the breakwaters of Port Elizabeth on the morning of 17 November 1942, just as the sun was lifting off the eastern horizon into a blue, untroubled sky. At the first push of the long Southern Ocean swell, the grey-painted merchantman gave a lazy roll that brought groans of protest from her riveted plates and sent unattended crockery crashing to the deck in her saloon pantry. On the bridge, Captain William Lorains grimaced and silently cursed the sea for this arrogant flexing of her muscles. He gave the order to bring the ship's head around to the south and took one last look at the slowly awakening city they were leaving astern.

After the rigours of a war-ravaged Britain and the long weeks of running the unseen gauntlet of the U-boats, South Africa had seemed like a taste of Paradise. The memory of the bright lights, the shops crammed with half-forgotten luxuries, and the lavish hospitality of the South African people would stay with Lorains for a long time to come. The return to the serious business of seafaring in wartime was not a prospect he relished, but it was an unavoidable necessity. He shrugged and turned to face the open sea, sniffing at the clean, salt air, consoling himself with the thought that it was at least a good day to go sailing.

The *Teesbank*, owned by the world-wide traders Andrew Weir & Co of London – familiarly known as the Bank Line, was a 5,136-ton motorship, built at William Doxford's yard at Sunderland in 1937. In her short pre-war career, she had worked the charter markets of the world and was as much at home in the China Sea as she was off this southern tip of Africa. On her present voyage, she was bound in ballast for Demerara, British Guiana, which lay 5,500 miles to the north-west. After rounding the Cape of Good Hope, her route would take her across the broad reaches of the South Atlantic, a largely benign ocean, ruffled only by the favourable South-East Trades, once the motive power of the windjammers of a bygone age. From the weather aspect, the passage promised to be idyllic.

As he set a course to pass clear of Cape Recife, whose the tall, black-and-white painted lighthouse was now visible to the west, forty-one-year-old Captain Lorains's thoughts were not only for the weather. Before sailing from Port Elizabeth, Naval Control had warned him to be on the look-out for U-boats off the Cape of Good Hope. It was known that a group of Type IXC long-range boats, accompanied by a U-tanker, had penetrated into the South Atlantic as early as mid-September and were creating havoc amongst unescorted merchantmen sailing the waters of the Cape. In the space of six weeks, twenty-four ships, totalling 103,164 tons, had been sent to the bottom, and pending the arrival of escort vessels from the UK, the slaughter seemed set to continue.

The *Teesbank*, which carried a crew of sixty-two including a party of DEMS gunners, was armed with the usual four-inch and twelve-pounder guns, two 20 mm Oerlikons, two .303 Vickers machine-guns and two .303 Marlins. In a gun-fight with a surfaced U-boat, she would be capable of giving a good account of herself. But she was unlikely to be given this opportunity: the days when a U-boat commander was prepared to challenge a ship on the surface were long past. The attack, if and when it came, would be unseen and from beneath the sea.

The weather held fine, and the *Teesbank*, taking advantage of the west-going flow of the Agulhas Current, was abeam of the Cape of Good Hope on the evening of the 18th. There had been no sign of the enemy, and it was with confidence that Lorains set out across the Atlantic. For the next eighteen days, until she closed the coast of South America, the *Teesbank* would be sailing in waters reputed to be free of U-boats.

Unknown to Lorains – or indeed to the Admiralty – the U-boats patrolling off the Cape had long since withdrawn into the South Atlantic. They were all running short of fuel and food, and many of them were down to their last torpedo. In late November seven of these boats were in mid-Atlantic clustered around a U-tanker which had been waiting to attend to their needs. Among the idling flotilla were *U-128*, commanded by

Korvetten-Kapitän Ulrich Heyse, and *U-159*, commanded by Kapitän-Leutnant Helmut Witte. Heyse, an ex-merchant seaman, and Witte were old friends, and they had much to discuss as they lolled on the surface waiting their turn to go alongside the tanker. The talk was not all of Berlin and *bierkellars*. Witte had recently sunk eight ships of 47,233 tons off the Cape and was well pleased with *U-159* and his crew. Heyse, on the other hand, had drawn a blank in that area and had been forced to cast his net further north. Off the Cape Verde Islands, a point of convergence for heavily laden ships bound for Britain from the Cape, West Africa and South America, *U-128* had met with only marginally better luck. Three ships of 15,571 tons were a disappointing score for such a long and arduous patrol.

With their stores and fuel replenished, *U-128* and *U-159* went their separate ways. Both boats were soon due to return to base, and – particularly *U-128* – were anxious to increase their score before the recall signal came. A week later they had crossed the Equator and were patrolling, out of sight of each other, in the region of St Paul's Rocks.

Penedo de São Pedro (St Paul's Rocks) lies fifty-five miles north of the Equator and 525 miles off the coast of Brazil. Devoid of vegetation and streaked white with the droppings of sea birds, the sixty-four-feet-high rocks are an awesome sight on an otherwise empty ocean. In the days of sail they sat square in the path of the windjammers bound to and from Cape Horn and the Cape of Good Hope and claimed many a victim. With the coming of steam and the ability of ships to choose their routes without reference to the fickle wind, St Paul's Rocks slipped back into a world of splendid isolation, the tumbling breakers on their blackened feet rarely sighted by the new breed of seamen. The advent of war in 1939, and the necessity for cargo ships to keep clear of coastal waters, had brought the rocks back into the path of hurrying civilization. The giant frigate birds which circle endlessly above St Paul's now witnessed unfamiliar plumes of smoke on the horizon as steamers passed on their errands of war.

At noon on 4 December, the *Teesbank* was abeam to the north-west of St Paul's Rocks, with only 1,500 miles to go to her destination. The weather was, as would be expected near the Equator, on the extreme edge of the South-East Trades, perfect

– blue skies, light winds, and the sea like a sheet of rippled glass. Given continuing fine weather, Captain Lorains estimated the *Teesbank* would be off Demerara on the night of the 10th, probably berthing on the morning of the 11th. With a full cargo to load, it seemed more than likely the ship would stay over Christmas in the port. This was a prospect welcomed by Lorains and his men, who, lulled by pleasant memories of South Africa and a passage which so far had been blissful, were having difficulty in associating themselves with the war. They were in another world.

The *Teesbank*'s luck was about to run out, for 240 miles due north of St Paul's Rocks *U-128* lay stopped on the surface, rolling gently in the long swell. Most of her crew were on deck enjoying the sting of the hot sun on their naked bodies. In the conning-tower, Ulrich Heyse, sweat staining the back of his thin shirt, stood contemplating the empty horizon. He was bitterly disappointed, for since leaving the rendezvous with the U-tanker, *U-128* had still not improved on her score of only three ships sunk. Soon – probably within a few days – her time in the Atlantic would be up and she would be recalled home. Heyse was desperately in need of a substantial target.

At ten minutes to three on the morning of the 5th, the bridge of the *Teesbank* was as quiet as a graveyard. The only sound that disturbed the stillness of the night was the measured thump of the four-cylinder Doxford engine as it drove the empty ship through the water at almost thirteen knots. In the starboard wing of the bridge, her second officer, with the last hour of his watch approaching, paced the deck with light footsteps, as though reluctant to disturb the slumbering magic of this tropical night. In the outboard corner of each wing of the bridge, where the slim barrels of the 20 mm Oerlikons silhouetted against the star-filled sky were a grim reminder of the war, a heavy-eyed DEMS gunner scanned the horizon with a marked lack of enthusiasm. In the darkened wheel-house, his face dimly illuminated by the soft glow from the compass binnacle, the Indian quartermaster might well have been mistaken for a sleeping statue, were it not for the occasional quarter turn he gave to the wheel to keep the ship on course.

The tranquility of the night was destroyed at precisely 02.52, when Ulrich Heyse's torpedo tore into the *Teesbank*'s after cargo hold and exploded with devastating effect. Captain William Lorains was out of his bunk and racing for the bridge ladder before the sound of the explosion had died. As he went up the ladder at a run, he heard the beat of the engine suddenly quicken and accelerate into a frenzied tattoo. Then, just as suddenly, it ground to a halt. Lorains needed no engineer to explain to him that the propellor shaft, which passed through the after holds, had been smashed by the explosion, severing the connection between engines and propellor.

By the time he reached the wheel-house, the ship was settling rapidly by the stern, and Lorains did not hesitate to give the order to abandon ship. Quickly and with the minimum of panic, the *Teesbank*'s four lifeboats were lowered to the water and boarded by her crew. Lorains and his senior officers stayed with the ship, but a few minutes after the boats had pulled away, Heyse put his second torpedo into the *Teesbank*. She began to go down, and Lorains had no alternative but to leave her.

At 03.41 the *Teesbank* went to her last resting-place in 2,000 fathoms, leaving her crew adrift and 700 miles from the nearest land. Providentially the sea was calm, but there the good fortune of the survivors ended. Two men had been injured by the second torpedo, one of them very seriously. The same explosion had so damaged one of the boats that it had to be abandoned, its occupants being distributed amongst the other boats. It also came to light that the first torpedo had brought down both main and emergency wireless aerials, and it had not been possible to transmit an SOS. The demise of the *Teesbank* had gone unannounced to the world over the horizon. No search for survivors would be set in motion until long after she was found to be overdue at Demerara.

Having watched his ship go down, Lorains took stock of the situation. The nearest land, the coast of Brazil in the region of Fortaleza, lay 720 miles to the south-west. The three lifeboats were well provisioned, and with the south-easterly breeze likely to hold steady, he calculated they could possibly reach the coast in twelve or fourteen days. It was a considerable voyage to undertake in open boats, but there was no alternative.

Dawn was breaking when they hoisted sail and set off to the south-west, running with the wind slightly abaft the beam. All went well for most of that day, but as evening was drawing in, the lifeboat in charge of twenty-year-old Third Officer John Milton began to drop astern. During the night Lorains held the other boats back as much as he could, but when daylight came on the 6th, Milton's boat was out of sight. Lorains decided to press on, hoping to reach land and send help for Milton.

Three days later, the two boats, containing between them forty-three men, had covered over 200 miles, at an average speed of three knots. For the awkward, heavily laden lifeboats, this was good progress, but the day had started with tragedy, when one of the injured men, an Indian deckhand, died and Lorains had the sad task of burying him at sea. Later in the day, when the sun was high, the boats were intercepted by *U-461*, returning from a special mission off the North American coast. Korvetten-Kapitän Steibler, after questioning the *Teesbank*'s survivors, handed over some food but, in return, took Captain Lorains prisoner. When the U-boat had gone on its way, the boats now in the charge of thirty-year-old Chief Officer I. McLean, again hoisted their sails and continued to the south-west. The double blow they had suffered that day did nothing to raise morale.

As William Lorains stepped into captivity aboard *U-461*, some 1,700 miles to the west-north-west the Cardiff-registered ship *East Wales* was forty miles out of Port of Spain, Trinidad, and steaming eastwards in convoy. It was a warm, cloudless day, an auspicious start to a voyage of nearly 11,000 miles which would take the ship across two oceans to the farthest reaches of another continent, where a long and hard-fought war was moving towards its climax.

On the battlefields of North Africa, German and Italian forces, under the command of General Erwin Rommel, reeled under a two-pronged assault whose size and ferocity threatened to sweep them into the sea. Montgomery's Eighth Army, having finally broken out of the stalemate of El Alamein, had rolled forward 1,500 miles and was hammering at the gates of Tripoli. On the morning of 8 November, 290,000 British and American troops had landed on beachheads stretching from Casablanca to Algiers. In less than two weeks they had established sovereignty over the whole of that coastline and were pushing eastwards to the Tunisian frontier. Overall, close on half a million Allied troops were engaged in the fast-moving struggle, and the task of keeping them supplied fell, in the main, to Britain's merchant ships. The *East Wales* was but one link in the supply line.

Built in 1925 by Dobsons of Newcastle, the 4,358-ton steamer was owned by Gibbs & Co of Newport and registered in Cardiff. Much of her life had been spent carrying coal out of the South Wales ports to the far corners of the earth, returning laden with grain or ores after long months in the cross trades of the Empire. Commanded by forty-seven-year-old Captain Stephen Rowland of Newport, she carried a crew of forty-five, including seven DEMS gunners. Her defensive armament consisted of one four-inch anti-submarine gun, two 20 mm Oerlikons and four Marlin machine-guns.

The *East Wales* had loaded a cargo of 7,000 tons of military stores in New York and, after calling at Port of Spain to receive routing orders from the Admiralty, was on her way to Alexandria, via Durban and the Suez Canal. For the first 400 miles out into the Atlantic, she was to enjoy the protection of a small convoy, but from then on she would be left to make her own way. On her long passage she would have to run the gamut of German, Italian and Japanese submarines, as well as the odd surface raider that cruised hungrily in her chosen path.

When the convoy dispersed on the morning of 11 December, Captain Rowland set an east-south-easterly course, in accordance with Admiralty instructions. This would take the *East Wales* to a point a hundred miles west of St Paul's Rocks, from whence she would head south-east to the Cape of Good Hope. The weather was set fine, with a light south-easterly breeze taking some of the heat out of the sun. At an average speed of 8.5 knots, Rowland expected to round the Cape on about 4 January and reach Durban, where the *East Wales* would call for coal bunkers, some four days later. It was a long haul and would include Christmas celebrated deep in the South Atlantic, in the region of the lonely island of St Helena. Rowlands hoped that, for his ship at least, the season of goodwill would extend well either side of Christmas.

The next forty-eight hours of the passage passed quietly, the *East Wales* bowling along at a speed in excess of eight knots and trailing her thick plume of smoke across a clear blue sky. Except for an hour of zigzagging around dawn and dusk – this on

Admiralty instructions, there was little to remind her crew of the bitter war waging far to the north. Then, on 13 December, Radio Officer Sydney Riley picked up faint cries for help from the Swedish cargo ship *Scania*, which was under attack by a U-boat near St Paul's Rocks, almost a thousand miles to the south-east. This was followed closely by a message from the Admiralty advising the *East Wales* to make a diversion to the north. The war was back on her doorstep.

Twenty-four hours later, nearly 400 miles to the south-east, the *Teesbank*'s two lifeboats under Chief Officer McLean were sighted by the American freighter *West Maximus*. When the forty-one tired and hungry men were picked up, they had been in the boats for nine days and had sailed 645 miles. No sign could be found of the other boat, and it was feared that Third Officer John Milton and his crew might have perished.

Milton and his men were, however, still very much alive, but a long way to the east. Light winds and the poor sailing qualities of their boat had slowed their progress to a mere 1½ knots, and in the nine days since the sinking of the *Teesbank* they had covered only 330 miles. Fortunately the nineteen men were in good shape, except for the fourth engineer, who had a broken collar bone, and they had not given up hope of reaching land.

By the afternoon of the 15th, the boat having progressed only thirty miles or so further to the west, John Milton was despondent. They were still nearly 400 miles from the land, and at the present rate of progress, that represented at least eleven days sailing. Would the food and, more importantly, the water last out that long? Who would be the first to go mad? Who would be the first to die? For a man just out of his teens, Milton was carrying an awesome responsibility, and as he sat at the tiller of his boat, he was acutely conscious of this unseen weight on his shoulders. When he saw the thin pencil of smoke on the horizon to starboard, he at first thought his eyes were playing tricks. Then, when a hoarse shout went up from a man in the bow, Milton jerked himself and his men into action. Oars were shipped and they put all their remaining strength into rowing towards the masts and funnel which had followed the smoke over the horizon. They might get only one chance like this. Milton broke out a smoke float.

At 15.45 Second Officer Andrew Dunn was idling away the closing moments of his watch on the bridge of the *East Wales*, enjoying the warm sun on his shoulders as he scanned the horizon. The sharp line between sea and sky was completely devoid of life. Minutes later, the masthead look-out reported a smudge of orange smoke dead ahead. Dunn reached for his binoculars. Very soon the distinctive red sail of a ship's lifeboat was visible from the bridge of the *East Wales*. Before sunset, the *Teesbank* survivors were on board, and John Milton was recounting the story of their eleven-day adventure to Captain Rowland.

The rescue of the *Teesbank*'s men brought home forcibly to Rowland the very real threat from U-boats that existed in the area, and he wasted no time in getting his ship under way again. Before doing so, however, he took the precaution of having the *Teesbank*'s lifeboat hoisted on board and re-stocked with food and water. As it turned out, this proved to be a largely futile gesture.

Throughout that night and all next day, the *East Wales* pushed south-eastwards, zigzagging around her mean course in order to spoil the aim of any lurking U-boat. Weather conditions were perfect, fine and clear, with a light south-easterly wind and slight sea. There was, however, a heavy swell, which gave the ship a slow, uncomfortable roll.

Helmut Witte, patrolling in *U-159* some 120 miles to the west-south-west of St Paul's Rocks, was anxiously awaiting the recall signal from Lorient. He was able to look back on what had been an arduous but, at times, immensely satisfying cruise. The 6,000-mile passage from Biscay to the Cape of Good Hope had proved to be a harrowing game of hide-and-seek but had been more than compensated for by the five action-packed weeks that followed in South African waters. During that time *U-159* had accounted for more than 47,000 tons of Allied shipping. But for the month just past there had been only the tedious and largely fruitless sweeping of the area in the vicinity of St Paul's Rocks. Since the meeting with the other boats at the refuelling point, *U-159* had sunk only two more ships, and the horizon was once again as empty as the Alster on a wet Sunday. Witte was more than ready to go home. Then, one hour before sunset on the 16th, the *East Wales* came steaming into sight, her tall funnel belching black smoke as Captain Rowland urged her on through the danger zone.

No one on board the *East Wales* saw the track of the torpedo which tore into her engine-room at precisely 17.25 and exploded with a deafening bang. The ship stopped dead in the water.

Andrew Dunn was in the mess-room taking an early dinner, a privilege accorded to those who kept the punishing middle watch. When he reached the deck, his ears ringing and the stench of burnt cordite in his nostrils, the ship was already settling by the stern, clouds of black smoke pouring through her engine-room skylight. Her funnel and both topmasts had fallen, littering her decks with a jumble of broken rigging and debris. Even as Dunn watched, the sea began to wash over the after deck.

Dunn looked around for Captain Rowland and the *East Wales*'s chief officer, Cecil London, but neither man could be seen. He assumed they were either still busy on the bridge or dead. It was up to him, as senior officer on the boat-deck, to take charge of the operation. He then discovered that the *Teesbank*'s lifeboat, which had been stowed ready provisioned on deck in case of such a catastrophe, had also been smashed by the explosion. There remained only one full-size lifeboat, two jollyboats – little bigger than dinghies – and two rafts to carry away sixty-four men, assuming they were all still alive.

The port lifeboat went down smoothly, fully manned, then Second Officer Dunn, assisted by Chief Engineer Edwin Lloyd, turned his attention to the jollyboats. Fifteen men were crammed into the port jollyboat, and this was also lowered without mishap. Lloyd and two able seamen then cleared away the starboard jollyboat, dropped it to the water and piled down the scrambling-net. Dunn was about to follow when it occurred to him that they were ill-prepared to face the challenge awaiting them once clear of the ship. The nearest inhabited land, the coast of Brazil, lay over 400 miles away, and to have any reasonable chance of reaching it they would need some navigational equipment, other than the boat's unreliable compass. At the very least, they must have a sextant with them. Although he was aware that the ship might sink at any moment, Dunn called to Lloyd to hold the boat alongside and ran for the chart-room.

Lying conveniently on the chart-room settee – probably left by Chief Officer London, who would have been preparing to take star sights when the ship was struck – Dunn found a sextant, a nautical almanac and a set of tables. He gathered them up and was about to return to the boat-deck when he heard the staccato sound of morse coming from the wireless-room. Flinging open the door, he found Chief Radio Officer Sydney Riley bent over the morse key calmly transmitting a distress call. This was a brave action, but to no avail. Riley was not aware that the explosion of the torpedo had brought down the *East Wales*'s topmasts, and with them her wireless aerials. Dunn shouted to Riley to give up his fruitless task and follow him to the boat. He could feel the deck of the ship beginning to slide under him.

Confident that the radio officer was behind him, Dunn scrambled down to the boat-deck and lowered the sextant and books into the jollyboat. He then jumped for the rope-falls, intending to go down hand-over-hand into the boat. But before he was half way down the falls, the *East Wales* gave a lurch and he was thrown against the ship's side and momentarily stunned. He lost his grip on the ropes and plummeted into the sea.

Fortunately for Andrew Dunn, the men in the boat acted swiftly, and he was hauled aboard before he could drift away. His first action when he regained his senses was to look around for Riley. The radio officer was nowhere to be seen.

There was nothing more to do but to pull away from the sinking ship, for the small boat would be in danger of being swamped when the *East Wales* took her last dive. The heavy swell made rowing difficult, but man's will to survive releases in him untapped sources of strength, and the oars were soon biting the water with a purpose. A helpful wave gave the boat a push, and they were out of danger. At that moment Sydney Riley who, true to the tradition of radiomen down the years, had stuck to his post to the last, appeared on deck, a forlorn figure alone on a doomed ship.

Dunn's first instinct was to take his boat back alongside, but this he dismissed as a foolish risk that might cost all of them their lives. He called to Riley to jump, but the radio officer, possibly because he could not swim, shook his head.

The other jollyboat, which was also lying off, now pulled towards the ship, its occupants signalling wildly for Riley to take his chance with the sea. As the boat drew near, the radio officer summoned up his last reserves of courage and vaulted over the rail into the sea. The mortally wounded *East Wales* chose that moment to break her back.

Clinging to the tiller of his boat, Andrew Dunn watched in horror as, with a terrible grating of steel on steel, the forward half of the vessel broke away and rolled to port before sinking. The after section followed, going down stern first. The port jollyboat, which was by then close in, was caught by the wreckage and dragged under. Neither the brave Sydney Riley nor the men who had sought to rescue him were ever seen again.

From the time she was torpedoed until she went down, the *East Wales* had lived a little over three mintues – albeit a long three minutes for those involved. When she was gone, swallowed up by the element she had fought and lived by for seventeen honourable years, she left wallowing in the flotsam-covered swell one lifeboat containing twenty-eight men, a jollyboat with thirteen on board and two rafts carrying six survivors between them. Ironically, all nineteen survivors of the *Teesbank* had survived this their second brush with death in eleven days. But of the men of the *East Wales*, Captain Stephen Rowland, Chief Officer Cecil London, Third Officer John Grogan, Third Engineer Leslie Appleton, Chief Radio Officer Sydney Riley and twelve others were missing. Thus Second Officer Andrew Dunn found himself in command of the survivors of two sunken ships.

There was no time for the thirty-one-year-old Yorkshireman to wrestle with the enormity of the task facing him, for *U-159* now came to the surface and motored slowly towards the boats. In the submarine's conning-tower eight men could be plainly seen, four of whom were manning machine-guns trained on the pathetic flotilla of boats and rafts. It appeared to Dunn that they were about to be shot down like dogs, but surprisingly he felt no fear, only sadness that he was to die so ignominiously after having survived thus far.

Dunn need not have feared for his life. In approaching with guns trained, Kapitän-Leutant Witte was merely taking a precaution against the possibility of hand-grenades being hurled at his submarine. The U-boat men regarded British merchant seamen with a healthy respect, even when they were in lifeboats.

When the U-boat was within hailing distance, Witte, who spoke fluent English, asked for the ship's captain and navigating officers. Dunn, who had no wish to be whisked off into captivity, made himself as inconspicuous as possible. Third Officer Milton of the *Teesbank*, the only other surviving navigator, did likewise. The remainder, realizing that their lives would depend on skilful navigation from there on, chorused in ragged unison that their captain and navigators had all gone down with the ship. Although Witte must have realized they were not telling the full truth, he seemed content to take them at their word. He compromised by then asking for details of the ship, her cargo and her destination. He received some very imaginative answers, none of them true, but again he seemed satisfied.

The two lifeboats drifted alongside the submarine, and Dunn took the opportunity to examine her closely. She appeared to be of about 700 tons and seemed freshly painted above the waterline. Her underwater part, which she revealed each time she rolled in the swell, was covered with barnacles and sea grass. She had been a long time out of dock.

After enquiring if there were any wounded and being told there were minor injuries, Witte ordered that bandages be passed to the boats. When this had been done, he said with the ghost of a smile on his face, 'As you unfortunately have no navigating officer, you had better steer south-west for 420 miles, until you come to Brazil.' As the U-boat prepared to depart, he shouted 'Merry Christmas!' adding, 'The name of your ship is the *East Wales*, and you were bound from New York to the Middle East with a cargo of war supplies – am I right?' No one in the boats answered but the looks on their faces spoke volumes. Under such circumstances, to be wished the compliments of the season was bad enough; to learn that someone, somewhere, had betrayed their ship seemed like a last, gross insult to those who had just given their lives.

The U-boat remained on the surface close by for some hours. Dunn assumed she was recharging her batteries. In fact, Witte was preparing his boat for the long passage back to Biscay. *U-159*, now with 59,372 tons of Allied shipping to her credit, had received the long-awaited recall to base.

When the submarine did finally motor away, Dunn collected the lifeboats and rafts together. In the choppy sea running, the six men on the rafts were suffering great discomfort, most of them being violently seasick. Dunn transferred four of those unfortunates to the larger boat and took the tiller of that boat himself. The two lifeboats and the rafts were then lashed together, and sea anchors streamed. Dunn's plan was to remain in the vicinity of the sinking until daylight, as there was a possibility, however remote, that Riley had been able to get away an SOS before he died, and a nearby ship might be on the way.

By dawn on the 17th, the two men on the rafts were in such a wretched state that Dunn had no alternative but to make room for them in the large boat. All stores and water were removed from the rafts and distributed between the two boats. The rafts were then cut adrift and, with the lifeboat towing the jollyboat, they set sail for land. Dunn's boat had thirty-six men on board, and the jollyboat, in the charge of Able Seaman Owens, had eleven. Both were uncomfortably crowded and with little freeboard. Fortunately, although the swell was still heavy, the sea decreased as the day wore on, and the boats sailed well, running free with a gentle south-south-easterly breeze abaft the beam.

The *East Wales* had sunk in position 00° 24'N 31° 27'W, and the nearest land, Capo de São Roque on the north-east coast of Brazil, was, as Helmut Witte had correctly stated, 420 miles to the south-west. Assuming the south-easterly breeze held good, Dunn estimated they would reach the coast in nine or ten days. The boats were well supplied with water, biscuits, pemmican, Horlicks tablets and chocolate. In addition, by some curious chance, they also had on board fifteen bottles of the finest West Indian rum. The journey would be tedious and uncomfortable, but the survivors were unlikely to expire from want of food and drink. However, from the start Dunn prudently set the twice-daily ration at three ounces of water, one biscuit, four pieces of chocolate, four Horlicks tablets and one teaspoon of pemmican per man. The rum he set aside for emergency use.

On the second day, Chief Engineer Edwin Lloyd, who was in the jollyboat, became desperately ill with seasickness, and it was necessary to transfer him to the lifeboat, which was riding the seas more easily. That left Dunn with thirty-seven men crammed into his boat, and the extra weight began to tell. From time to time the lighter jollyboat surged ahead on its towrope, overtaking the lifeboat. Both boats were very low in the water, and a collision might have caused disaster to either. On the morning of 19 December, the towline was slipped and the small boat allowed to sail independently, although Dunn instructed Owens to stay in sight.

The men's diet was also to cause Dunn trouble. As had been discovered before by so many who had ended up in lifeboats, the Horlicks tablets were sickly and thirst-provoking, while the pemmican was a vile concoction only the Board of Trade could have contrived to inflict on shipwrecked merchant seamen. As a small compensation, Dunn began issuing a tot of rum to each man in the evenings, but he was soon obliged to discontinue this. Although the spirit had a transitory uplifting effect on the men, it also greatly aggravated their thirst.

The light south-easterlies stayed with them for the next twenty-four hours, and the boats made good a speed of about two knots. But on the afternoon of 20 December the wind increased to force 4, bringing with it an angry sea. The jollyboat began to fall astern, and by nightfall, having lost sight of the smaller boat on two occasions, Dunn brought the towline back into use. Sun-sights taken that day had shown they were no more than five days from land, and Dunn felt confident enough to increase the rations to give an extra meal at noon. To those safe at home in Britain, some of whom had never ceased to grumble at the severity of food rationing, a dry biscuit smeared with sour-tasting beef extract would not have seemed a very exciting prospect, but to the forty-seven survivors of the *Teesbank* and *East Wales*, crowded into two small boats and adrift on an empty and increasingly hostile sea, the additional meal, however frugal and unappetizing, was like a shaft of sunlight through the dark clouds.

At 08.30 on the morning of 21 December, smoke was sighted on the horizon, and a fever of excitement swept through the boats. Orange smoke floats were broken out and set off, but it soon became apparent that they had not been seen by the passing ship. Fortunately the disappointment that followed was quickly dissipated when, later in the day, heavy rain fell. Dunn led the way by stripping off, and the others followed. Soon the survivors were revelling in the clean, cool rain as it sluiced down their naked bodies, washing away the dirt and salt of five days. As a tonic, this proved a far greater success than the rum.

Sails were used as rain-catchers, and sufficient water was

collected to replenish the fresh-water tanks of both boats. They were now, by Dunn's calculations, less than 200 miles from the coast and crossing the track of shipping steaming between the Cape and the Caribbean. This was confirmed next morning, when another column of smoke was sighted on the horizon. Again smoke floats were set off but, as before, they were not seen by the distant ship.

They continued sailing in a south-westerly direction, and when night closed in on them for the sixth time, their spirits were flagging. It was then that the miracle they had been praying for happened. At 19.40 bright lights were seen to starboard about eight miles off. Dunn had no intention of being ignored for the third time and shinned up the mast of the boat to light two red-hand flares. They must have been seen at once by the approaching ship, for she signalled back with her morse lamp. In less than an hour the survivors were being helped aboard the Swedish cargo liner *Glimarren*. They had been in the lifeboats for six days two hours and had covered 240 miles.

Twenty-four hours later the *Glimmaren* landed Second Officer Andrew Dunn and his men at the Brazilian port of Natal, close southward of Capo de São Roque. The exhausted but happy men spent a Christmas Day none of them would ever forget in Natal's Grand Hotel. Next day US Army planes flew them to New York to await a ship home.

Following their encounter with *U-461* and the taking prisoner of Captain William Lorains, the other survivors of the *Teesbank*, led by Chief Officer I. McLean were to spend six more days in their boats, before being picked up on 14 December by the *West Maximus* when only ninety miles from the land. They were put ashore in Rio de Janeiro eight days later.

The subsequent careers of *U-128* and *U-159* were short and largely unfruitful. The *Teesbank* was *U-128*'s last victim, for she was herself sunk off the Brazilian coast on 17 May 1943 in a combined attack by USS *Moffett*, USS *Jouett* and aircraft of US Squadron No.74. On her way back to base, *U-159* fell in with and sank the 5,449-ton British cargo ship *Lagosian* off the coast of Spanish Sahara. She was lost on her next patrol, being sunk in the Caribbean by aircraft of US navy Patrol Squadron No.32.

10   Caribbean Ambush

In the autumn of 1942, Axis naval planners estimated that, in order to dry up the flow of food and war materials into Britain, they would need to sink in excess of 700,000 tons of Allied shipping a month, every month, over a prolonged period. By the end of October, this target was beginning to look obtainable, ninety-three ships of more than 600,000 tons having been disposed of in that month. In November this increased to 109 ships of 729,160 tons, with the result that, although the enemy was not aware of it, he was sinking ships faster than American and British shipyards could produce them.

Hitherto, the great majority of these sinkings had taken place on the convoy routes of the North Atlantic, but as early as September a number of U-boats had begun to move further south, where the pickings were becoming rich. In addition to the Type IXCs operating off St Paul's Rocks, a pack of eight U-boats had gathered off the mouths of the Orinoco and were creating havoc amongst shipping on its way to and from the Caribbean. During the months of September, October and November, these modern-day buccaneers, confining their attacks to single, unescorted merchantmen (as had their flamboyant counterparts of the early eighteenth century) had sunk seventy-one ships of 215,000 tons.

It was against such a background that the 4,692-ton *Treworlas* sailed from Capetown on the morning of 30 November, bound for Trinidad with 3,000 tons of manganese ore. The *Treworlas*, which had a top speed of nine knots in favourable weather, seemed a likely candidate for the attentions of the U-boats.

Built in 1922 by Redhead & Sons at South Shields, the *Treworlas* was owned by the Hain Steamship Company of London. Like all her sisters, she was registered at the tiny

Cornish port of St Ives, which would have been hard pressed to accommodate one of her lifeboats. This idiosyncrasy dated back to the founding of the company by Captain Edward Hain of St Ives in the days of sail.

Although designed exclusively for world-wide tramping, the *Treworlas* had elegant lines, being flush-decked with tall masts and funnel and a smart clipper stern. In her heyday, painted in the distinctive black and white Hain Line colours, in appearance she had been able to hold her own with any cargo liner. In her drab, war-time grey, streaked with rust, she now had about her the air of an ageing, genteel lady fallen on hard times. Her crew of forty-seven included seven DEMS gunners, who manned her somewhat formidable armament of one four-inch, one twelve-pounder, one Oerlikon cannon and eight light machine-guns.

The sun was well up over Table Bay when the *Treworlas* steamed bravely out into the South Atlantic on that November morning. On her lower bridge, twenty-one-year-old Second Radio Officer Richard Webb rested his elbows on the forward bulwark rail and gazed in wonder at the long swells marching in on the ship from the horizon, glassy smooth but swollen with latent power. Despite the warmth of the sun on the back of his neck, Webb gave an involuntary shiver. The swells, he knew, would subside as the ship drew away from the land, but there were greater dangers still hidden beyond that distant horizon.

One deck above, in the wheel-house, Captain Thomas Stanbury, fifty-one years old and wise in the ways of the sea, cast a less jaundiced eye at the horizon. Summer in the South Atlantic would make for a pleasant passage, with light following winds, slight seas and blue skies dotted with tufts of fair-weather cumulus. This was 'flying-fish weather', and Stanbury revelled in it. His only cause for concern was that the *Treworlas*, with a great weight of ore stowed low down in her holds and beam-on to the south-easterly swell, would roll her way across the ocean like a Saturday night drunk. But after a few days, with everything moveable lashed down, even that would be bearable. As to the enemy, Stanbury had met him before and was prepared to meet him again.

The *Treworlas* was a thousand miles north-west of Capetown when, in the early hours of the morning of 5 December, the

Teesbank was torpedoed off St Paul's Rocks. Stanbury was unaware of this, but three days later he received an urgent radio message from the Admiralty warning of increased U-boat activity in the path of the *Treworlas* and advising a change of course.

Days, then weeks, passed without incident, and all the while the *Treworlas* steamed north-westwards at nine knots, flushing out silvery shoals of flying-fish with her bow wave, while a lone albatross untiringly criss-crossed her wake like a silent guardian angel. Day after day, the horizon remained empty of both friend and foe, and gradually a sense of well-being crept over the ship. With Christmas approaching, thoughts inevitably turned towards home and Christmases past. The celebration on board would be subdued but, the *Treworlas* having taken her stores in South Africa, there would be no shortage of good food and wine.

On the 16th the *Treworlas* was two days south of the Equator when, nearly 800 miles to the north-west, the *East Wales* met her end. At the same time, in the stormy waters of the North Atlantic, the ships of Convoy ON 153, bound from the UK to New York, were fighting for their lives against a pack of six U-boats led by Korvetten-Kapitän Johann Mohr in *U-124*.

When the battle was over and ON 153 cut to ribbons, Mohr decided to try his luck further south. *U-124*, a long-range Type IXB, had taken on contaminated diesel oil at her last refuelling and since leaving her base had been dogged by series of engine breakdowns. Mohr hoped that in the calmer waters of the Caribbean his problems would be eased.

French Guiana was abeam to port, with less than 600 miles to go to Port of Spain, when, on 25 December, the officers of the *Treworlas* gathered in the dining-saloon and raised their glasses in the traditional Yuletide toasts. They were on their roast turkey when the radio officer on watch entered the saloon and handed Captain Stanbury a message in a buff envelope. Stanbury tore open the envelope and frowned. The message contained Christmas wishes from the Admiralty in the form of yet another warning of increased U-boat activity ahead. When the dinner was over, Stanbury took his chief officer aside and quietly instructed him to ensure that the ship's life-saving appliances were in a high state of readiness.

During the course of his watch on the evening of the 27th, Radio Officer Richard Webb received two more Admiralty signals regarding U-boats sighted in the area. All the signs were ominous. The net was closing around the *Treworlas*.

At midnight, having handed over the watch, Webb went to his cabin below the bridge feeling distinctly uneasy. The night was hot and humid, and he knew he would get little sleep, but he stripped off and lay down on his narrow bunk, the danger threatening the ship running through his mind. The *Treworlas* was now nearing the east coast of Trinidad, having steamed 5,200 miles since leaving Capetown. Thus far, she had survived unscathed, with no sight or sound of the enemy, other than the recurring warnings over the ether. In a little more than twelve hours she was due to reach Port of Spain, but first she had to pass through the islands. Would the ambush be laid there – just before dawn perhaps? Webb checked that his lifejacket was lying handy on the settee and fell into a troubled sleep.

There was no sleep for Johann Mohr that night. *U-124* was on the surface and patrolling the twenty-five-mile-wide channel between Trinidad and Tobago. It was a bright moonlit night, with a calm sea and a light, cooling breeze. In more peaceful times, Mohr would have been happy to lean on the conning-tower rail, drinking in the sheer beauty of the warm night, but now the bright moonlight worried him. His boat was far too conspicuous on the surface, yet there was a pressing need to take risks. The curse of the contaminated fuel was still upon *U-124*, and through this she had missed a number of kills. Mohr was anxious to increase his score before he was forced to return to Lorient.

With little more than an hour to go before the coming of dawn would oblige *U-124* to submerge, Mohr was jerked out of the silent reverie into which he had fallen by the excited voice of one of his look-outs. Following the man's outstretched arm, he lifted his binoculars, his nerve-ends tingling. Silhouetted by the brilliant moonlight was a large ocean-going freighter approaching from the east. Mohr was smiling as he slammed the diving-alarm with the palm of his hand. This was one that would not get away.

The crash of an exploding torpedo brought Richard Webb tumbling from his sweat-soaked bunk wide awake. Without stopping to gather up his clothes. he made an instinctive lunge towards the doorway of the cabin. As he did so, the ship gave a heavy lurch to starboard, catapulting him out into the alleyway.

The *Treworlas* went over 20 degrees to starboard and stayed there, but Webb, ignoring the fact that he was naked and without his lifejacket, clawed his way to the wireless-room. As he struggled to open the heavy teakwood door, the ship gave a convulsive shudder and sank under him, drawing him down with it. Fortunately Webb was a strong swimmer, but his lungs were on the point of bursting before he broke free of the suction of the sinking ship and reached the surface.

At that moment Mohr, who had felled the *Treworlas* with one well-aimed torpedo fired from his stern tubes, brought *U-124* to the surface. He was anxious to secure details of his victim and be clear of the shallow waters before daylight came.

First man through the conning-tower hatch, Mohr looked around him, but the *Treworlas* was already gone, dragged under in less than a minute by the sheer weight of the ore in her holds. All that remained to be seen was a scattering of wreckage and a single liferaft, on which one survivor was crouching. Mohr started his diesels and headed for the raft. The lone survivor, thinking his frail craft was about to be rammed, hurled himself into the sea.

Had Mohr but known it, Richard Webb was treading water only six feet away from the submarine when she surfaced. Webb was still dazed but had the presence of mind to take in the details of the U-boat. She appeared to be about 350 feet long and had two guns on deck, but it was the insignia on her conning-tower that threw the young radio officer into a panic. In the half-light he mistook Mohr's edelweiss emblem for the Rising Sun and concluded that his ship had been sunk by the Japanese. He had heard stories of the Japanese machine-gunning survivors in the water and was not anxious to put them to the test. He let himself sink again and swam away under water.

When Webb re-surfaced, the submarine was out of sight, Mohr having given up hope of finding a survivor willing to talk to him. Treading water, Webb looked around but he could see no sign of life. It then occurred to him that he was in waters which normally teamed with sharks and that the sooner he found something to float on the better. He had been swimming for about half an hour when, just as the sky was lightening in the east, he came across three others clinging to a large piece of wreckage. Webb joined them, relieved that, if he had to die, at least he would not be alone.

The four men drifted for another two hours, while the sun lifted above the horizon and began to climb in the sky. The sea around them remained empty and, although no word was spoken, their greatest fear was that before long the cruising sharks would find them. At last, to their great joy, they sighted a wooden liferaft drifting close by. They swam to it and scrambled aboard, none of them conscious that they owed their good fortune to the foresight of the *Treworlas*'s chief officer. On Christmas Day, warned by Captain Stanbury of the growing U-boat threat, he had cast off the rope painters securing the rafts to the ship, thus allowing them to float clear when she sank.

A short while later, three more men were seen in the water and hauled on board. Although the raft was only six feet by nine, a rectangular wooden framework built around galvanized steel buoyancy tanks, it accommodated the six men in reasonable comfort but offered no protection from the sun or weather. With Richard Webb now were twenty-year-old Apprentice Edward Beyer, who had abandoned his raft in such a hurry at the approach of *U-124*, DEMS gunner Marshall Burdett, Able Seaman Joseph McCrae and two other ratings, a Palestinian and a Jamaican. Of the six, only Burdett, who had been on watch on the gun platform aft when the torpedo struck, was fully clothed. The rest were naked.

Although, as second radio officer, Webb had not really figured in the hierarchy on board ship, he was the only officer on the raft, and it fell to him to take charge. His first action was to institute a search for other survivors. They paddled around in the floating wreckage for some time but found no one. Eventually two other rafts were seen, one supporting three men alive and the other with a man on it who was either badly injured or dead. They were unable to get close enough to those rafts to establish communication. Elsewhere the sea appeared to be empty, and the awful truth was now clear: of the forty-seven men on board the *Treworlas*, at least thirty-seven had gone down with her. Fortunately their end must have been very quick.

Webb conferred with Beyer, and between them they established that the ship had been torpedoed about nine miles off the coast of Trinidad, in the region of Galera Point. Navigationally, their task was simple: merely to steer the raft in a southerly direction until they fetched up on the shore. The raft had no mast, but a suitable piece of wreckage was retrieved and erected. To this was lashed a square of yellow canvas found in the raft's gear locker. The wind was light from the north-east, and progress would be painfully slow, but they would be heading in the right direction.

Having set his tiny command in motion, Webb turned his attention to the all-important question of sustenance. An investigation of the raft's provision tanks proved to be a shock. Both tanks were leaking, and the drinking-water and food they contained had been contaminated by sea-water. In the absence of anything better, the water was still drinkable, but three tins of biscuits were saturated and had to be thrown overboard. Being unsure of how long it would take to reach land, Webb sensibly decided to ration each man to 1½ ounces of water, four pieces of chocolate, two Horlicks tablets and two biscuits per day. He resolved to issue no water on the first day.

At 09.30 that morning, when a flight of three aircraft was seen approaching, it seemed that Webb's plan for survival would not be needed. With fingers made clumsy by their haste, the men struggled to open a canister of distress flares, only to find the canister full of water, and the twelve flares it contained sodden and unusuable. The raft also carried six smoke floats, but these too had been immersed in water. Five of them failed to ignite, and when the sixth and final float flared up and smoke went billowing across the surface of the water, the aircraft had crossed over and were disappearing from sight.

Some 3½ hours later, the survivors were again galvanized into action by the sound of aircraft engines. A large formation of planes appeared flying at about 6,000 feet but, although they flew directly over the raft, to the pilots it was obviously no more than a speck of flotsam on the water. Without any means of signalling, Webb and his companions had no hope of being seen.

Things took a turn for the better late in the afternoon. The other raft, carrying three survivors, had drifted within shouting distance, and while standing up to communicate with the other men, Webb realized he could now see the shore. The tops of palm trees and roofs of houses were clearly visible, indicating they were no more than four or five miles off the land and could be ashore by nightfall. A few minutes later, it seemed there was no limit to their good luck when two seaplanes bearing American markings came in, flying low. The other raft succeeded in setting off a smoke float, and the aircraft immediately dropped lower and began to circle the rafts. Although the planes then flew off towards the land, the survivors were convinced they had been sighted. It must be only a matter of time before they were rescued.

It was then that it all started to go wrong. As the aircraft disappeared from sight, Webb's makeshift mast carried away, and all control over the raft was lost. The wind then backed to the west, and they began to drift away from the land towards the open sea. The real test for the *Treworlas* survivors was about to begin.

For the next three days they drifted aimlessly, often in sight of land but unable to make progress towards it. Fortunately the weather stayed fair and the sea calm. Perched on their precarious wooden platform only inches above the sea, the six men stayed dry but, being without clothes or shelter, sufferd the tortures of the damned from the hot sun during the day. To add to their discomfort and danger, sharks began to circle the raft, at times attempting to overturn it. They were later joined by ferocious barracuda, which hurled themselves out of the water in an effort to get on board.

Using the four steel stanchions of the weather screen as clubs, the men fought a running battle with shark and barracuda for hours on end. Soon their strength began to fail, for they had little food to sustain them. The biscuits were running short, and the chocolate and Horlicks tablets had become so contaminated with salt water that they were difficult for even starving men to stomach. The pemmican, which should have been the mainstay of their meagre diet, tasted so foul that no one would touch it. (One can only assume that the early polar explorers, who apparently thrived on the yellowish-brown dried meat paste, had been blessed with a more palatable brand than that issued to British merchant ships in the 1940s.) But in spite of all these adversities, the morale of most of the men on the raft remained high. Only the Palestinian and the Jamaican, in Webb's words, 'grumbled and complained the whole time'.

The raft must have been drifting back and forth with the tide directly under the patrol route of the US naval aircraft, for planes were continually flying over, some of them at low altitude. Unfortunately, apart from their now rather tattered strip of yellow canvas, the survivors had nothing with which to attract attention. They were not to know that the planes which had sighted them at the start of their ordeal had reported their position and that a rescue craft had set out to search for them that day. However, while the raft was being blown out to sea, the rescue boat was searching inshore and, after a few hours, when nothing had been found, gave up and returned to harbour. As far as the naval authorities ashore were concerned – somewhat prematurely it would seem, all hope had been abandoned for the survivors of the *Treworlas* by nightfall on 28 December.

Rescue, when at last it came, was largely a matter of good luck. At about 10.00 on the morning of 31 December, two ships, one large and one small, were sighted steaming in company on a course which would bring them close to the raft. Determined that this, possibly their last chance, should not be missed, Webb stood up on the raft waving Gunner Burdett's shirt – one of the few pieces of clothing they possessed. His effort, which all but exhausted him, was rewarded when the smaller ship, the US escort vessel *PC 609*, broke away from the passenger ship she was guarding and headed for the raft at speed. Five hours later Richard Webb and his five companions were landed at Port of Spain. For them the last day of 1942 had proved to be the best.

The three men from the other liferaft arrived in Port of Spain forty-eight hours later, having been picked up by an American submarine-chaser on passage to Barbados.

The sands of time ran out for *U-124* when, three months later, off the coast of Portugal, she attacked Convoy OS 45 and was herself sunk by the combined efforts of HMS *Stonecrop* and HMS *Swan*. Johann Mohr and his crew went down with their boat, joining Captain Thomas Stanbury and thirty-seven men of the *Treworlas* in the realm of Poseidon.

11   The Slaughter of the Tankers

On the morning of 28 December 1942, only a few hours and some fifty miles removed from the sinking of the *Treworlas*, a convoy conference was taking place in Port of Spain, Trinidad. In a smoke-filled room at the port naval headquarters were assembled the masters of nine British and Norwegian tankers, together with the commanding officers of the ships of the Royal Navy's B5 Escort Group, recently arrived from New York. There was apprehension in the air as the escort commander spelled out the dangers and pitfalls likely to be met with on the forthcoming voyage.

Convoy TM 1, carrying in its various tanks 25 million gallons of oil fuels, ranging from light crude to high-octane benzine, was shortly to set sail on a 3,500-mile voyage across the Atlantic and into the Mediterranean. The ports of discharge for the ships had not yet been disclosed, but their masters needed no crystal ball to tell them they were bound for the coast of North Africa. Seven weeks after the brilliant success of Operation Torch, British and American forces now had the remains of the Axis armies bottled up on the Tunisian peninsula, but Allied supply lines were stretched perilously thin. The priority need was for fuel for the many thousands of tanks, lorries and aircraft and the fleets of coastal craft involved in that massive sledgehammer operation designed to drive Rommel out of Africa once and for all. The message behind the escort commander's briefing was implicit. The convoy must go through.

The objective was beyond argument, but the question 'How?' was undoubtedly uppermost in the minds of the tanker masters as they made copious notes on the courses, speeds and signals to be used during the voyage. It was common knowledge that the

U-boats, determined to cut the Allied North African supply lines, were out in the Atlantic in force. Viewed in the light of this, the convoy's escort force, which consisted of the destroyer HMS *Havelock* and the Flower-class corvettes *Godetia*, *Pimpernel* and *Saxifrage*, looked pitifully inadequate. Air cover was to be provided by the Americans for the first twenty-four hours, but beyond that the skies would be empty for weeks to come.

Had those assembled at the TM 1 conference been privy to happenings on the far side of the Atlantic, their doubts as to the success of the venture would have been considerably raised. Under orders from Admiral Dönitz, the crack Delphin Group of six U-boats was speeding southwards to set up a patrol line between the Azores and Madeira, directly in the proposed path of the convoy.

Among those present at the conference on that morning was Captain John Andrews, master of the 9,807-ton British tanker *Empire Lytton*. Owned by the Ministry of War Transport and managed for the duration by Harris & Dixon Ltd of London, the *Empire Lytton* was registered in Middlesbrough. She was a new ship, having been completed earlier in the year at Haverton-on-Tees by the Furness Shipbuilding Company, Her bottom was not yet fouled and her engines not yet fatigued, so, as merchant ships go, she was capable of a good turn of speed. Her crew of forty-eight included seven DEMS gunners, who had in their capable hands a four-inch HA/LA gun, a twelve-pounder, four Oerlikons and two twin Marlin machine-guns.

Of all the ships in the convoy, the *Empire Lytton* could be said to be extremely well equipped to face up to the U-boats. Her only great disadvantage lay in her cargo, for she carried 13,590 tons of aviation spirit. She was, to all intents and purposes, a floating bomb, primed to explode at the slightest provocation. In times of peace, Andrews and his crew would have been treading a hazardous path as they crossed the Atlantic. In that vicious shooting war, their lives hung by an almost invisible thread.

Shortly after midday on the 28th, the escort ships having completed re-fuelling and re-storing, preparations were made for the convoy to get under way. It was then found that the corvette *Godetia*, which had arrived from New York with two boilers defective, was not yet ready for sea. At the same time, the

Empire Lytton and the Norwegian tanker *Vanja* were also experiencing problems in their engine-rooms. By 14.00, the escort commander, having delayed the sailing as long as he reasonably could, made the decision to leave without the two temporarily immobilized tankers. The ailing *Godetia* was detailed to stay with them to act as escort when they did finally get under way.

The main body of the convoy was already out of sight when the *Empire Lytton* and the *Vanja*, escorted by HMS *Godetia*, finally cleared Port of Spain. Their progress was slow, for one of *Godetia's* boilers was still out of action. The first indication of the enemy's presence came six hours later, when the three ships were off the island of Tobago. A patrolling Catalina sighted a U-boat on the surface only seven miles ahead of the three stragglers, and *Godetia* went in to attack at her best speed. By the time she reached the spot, the U-boat – in all probability *U-124* – had dived, and the corvette could do no more than drop a speculative pattern of depth-charges, with the inevitable negative result.

It was dawn on the 29th before the two tankers and their escort joined Convoy TM 1, which then formed up in extended order, steaming in four columns of two ships with one ship on the starboard wing. The *Empire Lytton* took up her allotted position as rear ship of the centre column. In view of the paucity of escorts, the high-octane carrier was as safe as she could be.

The next three days passed peacefully, as the convoy, steaming on a north-easterly course, moved deeper into the Atlantic. After the oppressive heat of Trinidad, the fresh headwinds they met with were most welcome but, combined with the prevailing adverse current, they considerably reduced the speed of the ships. Some of the older tankers, perhaps being pushed too hard, began to leave tell-tale trails of oil on the water – much to the disgust of the escort commander in HMS *Havelock*.

The year 1943 came in almost unnoticed, except for the good news that *Godetia* had at last completed repairs to her second boiler. Twenty-four hours later the seemingly fated corvette reported that the main transformer of her radar had burnt out and she had no means of repair or replacement on board. TM 1 had lost one of its precious seeking eyes.

But the difficulties within the bounds of the convoy were insignificant compared with those building up outside. On the afternoon of 3 January *U-514*, returning from a successful patrol off the West Indies, quite by chance found herself in sight of TM 1. Her commander, Kapitän-Leutnant Hans-Jurgen Auffermann, wasted no time in contacting Dönitz, reporting the tankers and their puny escort to be on a course of 070 degrees at nine knots. Auffermann was instructed to shadow the convoy, attacking it as and when he was able. Meanwhile the six boats of Delphin Group, still meticulously combing the waters between Maderia and the Azores, were ordered south at all speed.

On the evening of the 3rd, Captain John Andrews was relaxing in his cabin below the bridge of the *Empire Lytton*, blissfully unaware of the threatening danger. The ship was in mid-ocean, roughly halfway between Trinidad and the Azores and was, in Andrews' opinion, barring the unlikely appearance of a German surface raider, relatively safe from attack. For the next few days, at least, he felt he would be able to take things easier, to shift some of the burden of command temporarily onto the shoulders of his officers. He might even be lucky enough to enjoy several nights of uninterrupted sleep. This he was in need of, for when the *Empire Lytton* drew near the Canaries, she would be once more entering the lion's den.

Chief Officer Alfred Baughn, keeping watch on the bridge, was similarly contemplating a peaceful interlude. It was a fine night, and Baughn was contentedly pacing the starboard wing of the bridge, occasionally lifting his binoculars to check that the *Empire Lytton* was not closing up on the ship ahead of her in the column, the 8,093-ton motor tanker *British Vigilance*. At 18.45, as Baughn was examining her dark outline through his glasses, the *British Vigilance* erupted in a sheet of flame. Hans-Jurgen Auffermann had made the first kill.

When Andrews reached the wheel-house seconds later, he found that Baughn had already ordered the helm hard to starboard and that the ship was swinging to clear the funeral pyre of the *British Vigilance*. Andrews took over, bringing the *Empire Lytton* back on course when she was clear of the blazing tanker. As he completed the maneouvre, he caught sight of the low outline of a surfaced submarine close on the port bow, etched in stark silhouette by the leaping flames.

Acting out of pure instinct and with no thought for the highly volatile cargo below decks, Andrews hauled the ship around to port and headed straight for the submarine, with the intention of ramming. Hans-Jurgen Auffermann acted with equal alacrity. Dark clouds of smoke billowed from *U-514*'s exhausts, and she shot across the *Empire Lytton*'s bows from port to starboard, clearing the tanker's stem by no more than twenty yards.

But *U-514* was not to escape completely unharmed. In the *Empire Lytton*'s starboard bridge wing, sixteen-year-old Apprentice Basil King, with barely six months sea service to his name, strapped himself into the Oerlikon harness and opened fire as the submarine cleared the bow.

Auffermann had by now worked his diesels up to full power and was running away from his assailant at fifteen knots, but that was not fast enough. Basil King's aim was good, and the 20 mm cannon shells began to slam into *U-514*'s conning-tower. Simultaneously the tanker *Norvik* opened fire with her four-inch, bracketing the submarine with her first two shots. Auffermann, very wisely, decided the time had come to crash-dive.

Despite the tension of the moment, Andrews had found it difficult to refrain from cheering as the Oerlikons shells riddled the U-boat's superstructure. Of the 30 rounds fired by King, at least two-thirds had found their target. It was only when Andrews saw two ominous splashes under the U-boat's stern that he gave thought to the danger of torpedoes. he increased speed and zigzagged violently away from the scene. Another two hours were to pass before the *Empire Lytton* rejoined the convoy, taking the place of the missing *British Vigilance* in the lead of the centre column.

The remainder of the night passed without further attack, but early next morning HMS *Havelock* picked up radio signals on her HF/DF which indicated a U-boat near by. *Godetia* was sent on an offensive sweep in the direction of the signals but found no sign of the enemy. *U-514* had withdrawn to a safe distance but was still shadowing the convoy and reporting to Dönitz by W/T.

To add to his burden, the Escort Commander was now faced with another pressing problem. All the escort ships were running low on fuel, and it would be necessary for them to replenish their tanks within the next forty-eight hours. Ample fuel for this purpose was on board the *Norvik*, which carried pipes for oiling at sea. *Havelock* was first to go alongside the tanker but, after she had taken on board only six tons, heavy seas forced her to abandon the operation. The escort commander then decided to alter course to the north, in order to reach calmer weather. This proved to be an unfortunate move, for it unwittingly brought the convoy nearer to the searching Delphin Group. At 15.00 on 8 January *U-381*, commanded by the grandiosely named Kapitän-Leutnant Wilhelm-Heinrich, Graf von Pückler und Limpurg, sighted the tankers and immediately alerted all U-boats in the vicinity.

When darkness came that night, Convoy TM 1 was 550 miles to the west of the Canary Islands. The weather was fine and clear, with a light south-easterly breeze, smooth sea and moderate swell. On the bridge of the *Empire Lytton*, Chief Officer Alfred Baughn had the watch, but Captain Andrews was hovering in the wheel-house, uncomfortably aware that conditions were ideal for a U-boat attack.

Had John Andrews been acquainted with the state of readiness of TM 1's escorts, his discomfort would have been even greater. *Havelock*'s HF/DF was working only intermittently, *Godetia*'s radar was, of course, still out of action and the corvette *Pimpernel*'s radar had also developed a serious fault. At that critical moment in the voyage, the long-range eyes and ears of the small escort force were partially closed.

The wolves closed in at 19.45, with *U-436*, commanded by Kapitän-Leutnant Günther Seibicke leading the pack. Seibicke fired three torpedoes in quick succession, hitting the Norwegian tanker *Albert L. Ellsworth* and the British tanker *Oltenia II*. Andrews, watching from the bridge of the *Empire Lytton*, saw the *Ellsworth* catch fire and the *Oltenia* sink like a stone.

The battle continued throughout the night, with the escorts, led by *Havelock*, fighting a magnificent defensive action. For many hours they held the U-boats at bay, but at 03.15 on the 9th the wolves again broke through the thin grey cordon, and in the following fifteen minutes the 6,833-ton *Minister Wedel* and the 10,034-ton *Norvik* were hit. Fortunately these ships did not catch fire, and it seemed possible that, if they were not further attacked, they might be salvaged.

An hour later it appeared that the determined depth-charge

attacks of the escorts had had the desired effect, for the U-boats withdrew and all went quiet. At 04.25, satisfied the danger had passed, even if only for a while, Andrews left Chief Officer Baughn in charge of the bridge and went below to his cabin. As he was lowering his exhausted body into a comfortable chair, unseen in the darkness to starboard of the *Empire Lytton*, Korvetten-Kapitän Hans-Joachim Hesse was maneouvring *U-442* into position for attack. A few minutes later one of the two torpedoes fired by Hesse struck the tanker on her starboard bow.

In the master's cabin the sound of the exploding torpedo was muted, but Andrews felt the shock and heard the screech of rending metal. His tiredness forgotten, he leapt from his chair and headed for the bridge, expecting that at any moment his ship and her 3 million gallons of high octane would turn into an ascending fireball, taking his charred ashes with her.

On reaching the bridge, Andrews found that the whole structure was covered in sticky, black fuel oil, as a result of which he was able to revise his thoughts of an early cremation. The indications were that the torpedo had hit in the *Empire Lytton*'s forward fuel tank and had been smothered by the thick oil. He rang the engines to stop and sent Baughn forward to assess the damage.

As he leaned over the bridge front peering into the darkness ahead, Andrews heard desperate cries for help coming from the main deck. He went below to investigate and found the ship's carpenter, John Little, lying on the deck with both legs broken. Fearing that the ship might already be sinking, Andrews ordered two seamen to put the injured man into one of the starboard lifeboats and to lower the boat to the water. In the darkness and with panic never very far below the surface, the boat was hurriedly lowered with the groaning carpenter lying on the thwarts. Being soaked in fuel oil, the rope falls were difficult to handle, and the forward one ran away. The boat tipped and was left hanging vertically from the after fall. John Little, helpless to save himself, was catapulted into the water and disappeared before any attempt could be made to save him.

Saddened by this tragedy, for which he felt partly responsible, Andrews returned to the bridge, where he was joined by his chief engineer, Fletcher Canning, who had left the engine-room to seek information. While the two men were discussing the situation, Baughn returned with the news that the damage forward was extensive but by no means fatal. The torpedo had struck just abaft the stem, blowing a hole roughly ten feet by four in each side of the bow; the forecastle head was in ruins, and the collision bulkhead had been breached. Fortunately there had been no outbreak of fire, but the ship was making water forward, although she seemed to be in no immediate danger of sinking. After some discussion with Baughn and Canning, Andrews decided it would be safer to abandon ship temporarily and to lie off in the boats until daylight.

With the weather being fine and the sea calm, the operation of abandoning ship should have gone smoothly, but the darkness and the slippery oil which covered everything between them produced a disaster. Baughn's lifeboat capsized on launching, throwing its occupants into the sea. Although his own boat was already full, Andrews immediately began to search the area for survivors. Dawn was breaking before he picked up the first man. Eleven others were eventually found, including Baughn, who was unconscious. The chief officer was hauled on board and for over an hour given artificial respiration, but without result. Alfred Baughn was dead.

Andrew's lifeboat now held twenty-three men and was very much overcrowded. Although he could see at least six others in the water and could hear the shouts of more, he was unwilling to risk another capsize. It was now full daylight and he decided that the most sensible course would be to return to the ship and off-load the men he had. On the way back to the *Empire Lytton*, he came up with the only other lifeboat which had been successfully launched. It was in the charge of Second Officer Ronald Moore and held eight men. Andrews instructed Moore to pick up the men in the water and carried on with his heavily laden boat to the ship.

The *Empire Lytton* was re-boarded shortly after 08.00, and Andrews and his men were able to clean the oil off themselves and put on dry clothes. The ship was now five feet by the head but otherwise seemed seaworthy. The corvette *Saxifrage* then appeared alongside and delivered an ultimatum. Unless Andrews was able to get his ship under way quickly and proceed at eight knots, the *Saxifrage* would be obliged to sink her by gunfire.

The last thing Andrews wanted was to lose his ship now, and in a desperate bid to postpone the decision, he persuaded the commander of the corvette first to search for the *Empire Lytton*'s other lifeboat and any men who might still be in the water.

When *Saxifrage* had reluctantly steamed away, Chief Engineer Canning went below to examine the possibility of raising steam. On returning to the bridge, the Chief reported he felt confident of producing up to eight knots, but certainly no more, *Havelock* had now arrived on the scene and was pressing Andrews for a decision. *Saxifrage* then returned with Second Officer Moore's boat in tow but had found no other survivors. While Moore and his men re-boarded the *Empire Lytton*, the two warships hovered within easy gun range, their signal lamps chattering.

Andrews appreciated that the hard-pressed escorts were anxious to dispose of the crippled *Empire Lytton* in order to concentrate their resources on the undamaged tankers, but he was not about to give up his ship so easily. He sent Canning below to raise steam and to re-assess the ship's capability after that had been done. Within half an hour, Canning returned grim-faced to report that the damage in the engine-room was worse than he had at first thought. He would be unable to give Andrews more than six knots. At 09.30, for the second and last time that day, the *Empire Lytton* was abandoned, her crew being taken off by HMS *Saxifrage*.

The escort commander now decided to leave the *Empire Lytton* to her fate, and *Havelock*, with *Saxifrage* in company, steamed off at full speed to rejoin the remnants of the convoy. Andrews stood on the deck of *Saxifrage* until his ship was out of sight, reflecting on the bravery of his men, whose valiant efforts had come to naught. Basil King, the sixteen-year-old apprentice, who should have been wielding nothing more lethal than a sextant, had manned the Oerlikon like a veteran gunner. Second Engineer John Bentley, Greaser Murray and Fireman Reid, the watch in the engine-room when the torpedo struck, had remained calmly at their posts until ordered up on deck. An Estonian deckhand, whom Andrews knew only as Herman, had for two hours supported Chief Officer Baughn in the water. Of the forty-seven men he had set sail with from Trinidad twelve days earlier, only thirty-one remained. Alfred Baughn was dead and fifteen, including the courageous Fireman Reid, were missing, believed drowned. As Andrews sadly turned away to go below to *Saxifrage*'s wardroom, he saw a flash and clouds of black smoke mushrooming up from the horizon in the direction of the *Empire Lytton*. Now he had lost his ship.

While *Saxifrage* was hurrying back to join the convoy, the U-boats were disposing of the other crippled and abandoned tankers. Kapitän-Leutnant Herbert Schneider in *U-522* sank the *Norvik* and the *Minister Wedel* between 12.00 and 14.00, while *Seibecke* in *U-436* returned to finish off the *Albert L. Ellsworth* at 17.43.

When *Saxifrage* caught up with Convoy TM 1 after dark on the 9th, it was a pathetic sight. Only the *British Dominion*, the *Vanja* and the *Cliona* remained intact and, urged on by *Havelock*, were steaming to the north-east at their best possible speed.

The massacre of TM 1 was not yet complete. After dark on the 10th, the U-boats returned, sensing a victorious climax to their operation. Four boats penetrated the escort screen on the surface, and despite the valiant efforts of *Havelock* and her consorts, the *British Dominion*, fully loaded with aviation spirit, went up in a ball of fire. Torpedoes were also fired at the *Vanja* and the *Cliona* but fortunately missed.

There is little doubt that, but for the arrival on the 11th of a Catalina flying-boat and three additional escort ships, TM 1 would have gone down in history as the convoy that sailed into oblivion. As it was, seven ships of 56,453 tons, carrying nearly 80,000 tons of oil, had gone to the bottom. Not one U-boat had been lost.

The *Empire Lytton* did not go as easily as Andrews had assumed. The smoke he had seen on the horizon was the result of an attempted *coup de grâce* by *U-442*, but the tanker was still afloat five hours later. It cost Hesse yet another precious torpedo before, at 18.38, the *Empire Lytton* took her final plunge.

U-442 outlived the *Empire Lytton* by just over a month. Her only other victim was the 7,176-ton US cargo ship *Julia Ward Howe*, which she sank north of the Azores on 27 January. Two weeks later she was caught on the surface in the western approaches to the Mediterranean by aircraft of 48 Squadron and sent to the bottom.

12   To the Bitter End

Leonardo da Vinci, the fifteenth-century artist and scientist, was a man of exceptional talents and, unusually for one of his kind, also of great humility. His last words before he died in 1519 were said to be: 'I have offended God and mankind because my work did not reach the quality it should have.' For a man who produced, amongst other things, the Mona Lisa and plans for the first helicopter, this was modesty indeed. What would da Vinci have thought of the works his name was to be associated with four centuries after his death?

Shortly before midnight on 13 March 1943, the 21,516-ton Canadian Pacific liner *Empress of Canada* was 350 miles off the coast of Liberia, sailing unescorted from the Middle East to the United Kingdom. She had on board 1,890 service personnel and crew. It was a black night and the great ship's frothing wake cut an erratic swathe through the tranquil sea as she zigzagged at full speed around her mean course. Her evasive action was to be of no avail for, on the stroke of midnight, as the watches were changing, a torpedo tore into her engine-room and she came slowly to a halt. The Italian submarine *Leonardo da Vinci*, commanded by Capitano di Corvette Gianfranco Gazzana-Priaroggia, after a fruitless month patrolling those equatorial waters, had at last found a target. Once the liner was crippled, it was easy for Priaroggia to finish her off. When she sank, she took 370 men with her. Several survivors died of shark-bites after rescue.

As the waves closed over the *Empire of Canada* and she began her slow, spiralling plunge to the bottom, another British ship was 1,600 miles to the south-west and following in the liner's invisible wake. The 7,628-ton *Lulworth Hill* was, however, a far cry from the faded opulence of the late *Empress of Canada*.

Owned by the Counties Ship Management Company of London
and built in 1940 by William Hamilton of Port Glasgow, she was
in outward appearance a modern tramp ship but, quite out of
character, was capable of a top speed of fourteen knots. She
carried a crew of forty-eight including seven DEMS gunners,
and was commanded by Captain William McEwan. Her
armament consisted of the usual four-inch gun on the poop,
four Oerlikons, two twin Marlin and two single Lewis
machine-guns and an early form of multiple rocket-launcher
known as a 'Pillar Box'. In addition – and this most unusual for a
merchant ship – she carried three depth charges at her stern
rail; how she was to use them without doing herself serious
harm was a matter for some conjecture.

Deep laden with 10,190 tons of raw sugar, 400 tons of rum
and 410 tons of fibre, the *Lulworth Hill* had left Capetown on
the morning of 11 March, bound for Freetown, where she
would join a convoy for the UK. The weather in the South
Atlantic was at its autumn best, with the South-East Trades
light and playful, the skies blue and the sun warm. There had
been no warnings of U-boats operating in the area and,
steaming at full speed along the route recommended by the
Admiralty, Captain McEwan anticipated a trouble-free passage,
arriving in Freetown some time on the 20th. At first it seemed
that this was not to be. Twenty-four hours out of Capetown, the
Lulworth Hill's radio officer intercepted a message from an
American merchant ship torpedoed not many miles ahead of the
British ship's position. McEwan put his guns' crews and
look-outs on the alert and began zigzagging.

But for the *Lulworth Hill* the tranquillity of the South Atlantic
remained undisturbed, and for the next six days she steamed
north-westwards unmolested, though still maintaining her
precautionary zigzag. Then, at dusk on the 18th, when she was
500 miles north-east of St Helena, an alert look-out spotted the
track of a torpedo racing in on the starboard side. There was no
time to take avoiding action, but fortunately the torpedo passed
harmlessly astern of the ship.

Captain McEwan hit the bridge at the first shrill call of the
alarm bells and was in time to see a submarine break the surface
not more than 250 yards on the starboard bow. In the
lengthening shadows of the oncoming night, the long, grey

shape, shedding water as it rose, had the appearance of a frightening sea-monster of the legends of old.

McEwan took the only action open to him, bringing his ship hard round to port and presenting her stern to the danger. The *Lulworth Hill*'s gunners, already closed up on the four-inch, acted with equal speed, opening fire on the submarine as soon as their gun came to bear. Their aim was accurate but, as the target was so close to the ship, they were unable to depress their gun sufficiently to score a hit. However, the two rounds they fired were to good effect, for the submarine immediately crash-dived. The *Lulworth Hill*, her engines making maximum revolutions and zigzagging with renewed zeal, made off in a south-easterly direction, seeking the cover of the night. At the same time, her radio officer was tapping out the all-too-familiar 'SSS', informing all ships that she was under attack by a submarine.

Below the waves, Capitano Priaroggia checked the *da Vinci*'s dive and levelled off at 20 metres. The Italian commander was visibly shaken at the short shrift he had received at the hands of an apparently helpless merchantman. At his side in the control room, the *da Vinci*'s German liaison officer was furious. To him, the simple operation had been an example of Italian bungling at its worst.

The SS officer had good reason to be concerned at the loss of an easy target, for, at that stage of the war, things were going disastrously wrong for the Axis Powers. On the Russian Front, twenty-two Wehrmacht divisions, led by Field Marshal Paulus, had only a few weeks earlier been forced to surrender at the gates of Stalingrad. In the Western Desert Rommel's army was in full flight, while in the Pacific the Japanese had at last been prised out of Guadalcanal by the Americans. But perhaps the most bitter pill Germany had had to swallow was the determined and successful assault being made on her main industrial cities by RAF Bomber Command. Up to 400 aircraft a night were laying waste to the Ruhr with thousands of tons of high explosives and incendiaries. The Luftwaffe, owing to its massive commitments in the Soviet Union and the Mediterranean, no longer had the resources with which to mount retaliatory attacks on British cities.

The *Lulworth Hill* had been steaming at full speed for an hour before the *Leonardo da Vinci* caught up with her. By then it was fully dark, with the moon obscured by cloud and with a fresh south-easterly blowing. The enemy submarine revealed her presence to the men on the bridge of the merchantman when she, somewhat unwisely, used a small searchlight to sweep the sea around her. McEwan passed the order for the gunners to hold their fire and, being careful to avoid stirring up a tell-tale wash, stealthily altered course until the *Lulworth Hill*'s stern was again to the submarine and she was moving rapidly away from her. The game of cat-and-mouse was on.

For another fifteen minutes the Italian submarine's searchlight continued to probe the darkness, while the *Lulworth Hill* fled to the south-west with her boiler safety-valves tightly screwed down. Another hour passed and McEwan, his eyes drawn through constantly scanning the horizon astern with binoculars, began to entertain hopes of a successful getaway. Then, at around 23.00, snowflakes rockets soared into the sky about five miles astern, turning night into day. The *Leonardo da Vinci* had not given up the chase. Fortunately the *Lulworth Hill* was far enough away to be still in the shadows, and McEwan again wisely restrained his gunners from firing.

Midnight came and went with no watches being changed, for every man of the merchant ship's crew was standing to at action stations – and had been so for four hours past. As the night wore on and the tension eased, McEwan deemed it safe to send some of his men below to rest, but leaving the guns fully manned and the look-outs doubled up.

At 03.45 on the 19th, in the darkest hours before the dawn, when life is said to be at its lowest ebb, the silence of the night was rent by a tremendous explosion, and the *Lulworth Hill* was brought up short and listing heavily to starboard. Capitano Priaroggia had found his mark.

The *Lulworth Hill*'s carpenter, Kenneth Cooke, was one of those asleep in his cabin when the torpedo struck. The force of the explosion blew him out of his bunk and, dazed and shaken, he had just regained his feet when the second torpedo ripped open the ship's side. Cooke, who had turned in fully clothed, stopped only to snatch up his lifejacket before making for the deck at a run.

Both torpedoes had hit forward of the bridge, breaking the

Lulworth Hill's back. By the time Cooke reached the boat-deck, the main deck was awash and he had only a few seconds to struggle into his lifejacket before jumping clear of the sinking ship.

In spite of the buoyancy provided by the lifejacket, Cooke found himself drawn down by the suction of the ship as she plunged bow first. He fought his way to the surface to find himself looking up at the stern of the ship as it lifted high in the air, the propellor still turning lazily. Then, in the grip of the increasing suction, he was dragged under again. When he broke the surface for the second time, the *Lulworth Hill* was gone.

It had taken less than two minutes for his ship to sink, and Cooke knew there could have been no time to launch lifeboats. He gave thanks for the sixth sense that had made him reach for his lifejacket before leaving his cabin but, at the same time, despite the warmth of the tropical water, he felt a cold fear creeping over him, for he knew that the ship had gone down over 700 miles from the nearest land. Was he alone in that great, empty ocean?

Looking around him in the inky darkness, with the waves spitefully slapping at his face, Cooke tried unsuccessfully to visualize in his mind's eye a distance of 700 miles. He soon gave up and turned his racing thoughts to how long his lifejacket would keep him afloat. Forty-eight hours, perhaps? And then he remembered the sharks. There was no shortage of them in that area; he had seen them from the deck of the *Lulworth Hill* – great hammerheaded brutes. He began to panic and struck out towards the spot where the ship had gone down. There must be something of her left – a hatchboard or a piece of wreckage on which he could take refuge – anything to get his legs out of the water.

A lesser man than Kenneth Cooke might have gone quietly mad there and then, but Cooke was not only of that particular breed of Englishman to whom a seemingly hopeless situation presents a challenge, he was also blessed with good luck. Within a few minutes he had found a cork lifebuoy, a fragile enough support, but it gave him an increased sense of security. Pushing it before him, he swam on and was overjoyed to see the red glow of a lifejacket light bobbing on the waves ahead. Soon he was drifting side by side with another survivor, Able Seaman Hull, one of the *Lulworth Hill*'s DEMS gunners.

With the sea lashing at their faces and, by its sheer persistence, threatening to drown them, the two men somehow managed to discuss the awful predicament in which they found themselves. Hull confirmed Cooke's assessment that there had been no time to launch the boats. Their only real hope, they decided, lay in finding one of the ship's liferafts, which were designed to float clear when she sank. They were about to begin their search when they sighted a small cluster of red lights on the surface not more than fifty yards off. They were not alone after all.

The two men were swimming towards the lights when, with a loud hissing of compressed air, the submarine surfaced between them and their goal. A searchlight was switched on and began slowly to sweep the sea. Accepting that life in a prisoner-of-war camp would be infinitely preferable to death by sharks or drowning. Cooke and Hull struck out towards the light.

Cooke's movements were hampered by the lifebuoy, which he was reluctant to adandon, and consequently Hull reached the submarine several minutes before him. Two of the crew heaved the gunner on board, and by the time Cooke found a handhold on the submarine's casing, Hull had been taken below.

Before he had time fully to recover his breath, Cooke was blinded as the searchlight was turned on him, and he heard a voice from the conning-tower demanding the name of his ship. Buffeted against the hull of the submarine by the waves and half-drowned, he had no will to answer other than truthfully. His questioner, whom he could vaguely make out leaning over the edge of the conning-tower, appeared to be wearing a naval uniform and spoke English with a strong German accent. Cooke assumed him to be the U-boat's commander. He was, in fact, being questioned by the *Leonardo da Vinci*'s SS liaison officer, temporarily assigned to the submarine for the express purpose of stiffening the resolve of the Italians which, at that stage of the war, was showing signs of crumbling.

The German fired question after question at the unfortunate Cooke, who was at such a disadvantage that he was obliged to answer to the best of his ability. Then the questioning suddenly stopped and the searchlight swung away to resume probing the darkness around them. The beam picked out what seemed to be a liferaft with several figures clinging to it and held steady. Without warning, the submarine's diesels thundered into life, and she surged forward. Cooke, taken by surprise, was dragged through the water at an ever-increasing rate. His arm, which was through a hole in the casing, felt as if it was being wrenched off at the shoulder, and his head went under water. After several agonizing minutes, which seemed like an hour in purgatory, he freed himself and, more dead than alive, was thrown clear by the submarine's wake and came gasping to the surface.

In desperation, Cooke swam after the submarine and came up with it when it stopped and played its searchlight over an upturned lifeboat, on which six men had taken refuge. Not wishing to repeat his earlier experience, he trod water when he was within twenty-five yards of the enemy and awaited the turn of events. From low in the water the submarine appeared to be huge – almost 250 feet long, he estimated. She had a very tall periscope or mast, a large-calibre gun forward of the conning-tower and a curious square structure aft, which could have been a seaplane hanger. Cooke had studied photographs of German U-boats, and she did not match up with any he had seen. He assumed she must be Italian, although the German accent of the man he took to be her commander puzzled him.

Cautiously Cooke moved closer, for he could now hear the same guttural voice berating the men on the keel of the lifeboat. For some time the man ranted against the RAF's bombing of German cities, and his voice rose to a scream with the words: 'Now you will drown!' Then the searchlight was abruptly switched off, the submarine's diesels again rumbled into life and she slipped away into the darkness. As the throb of her engines died away and a silence disturbed only by the slap, slap of the waves descended on the sea, the awful reality of his position came back to haunt Cooke. He was alone in a dark, hostile world, and his chances of survival were very, very slim.

But once again, in the face of adversity, Kenneth Cooke refused to be beaten. Pushing his precious lifebuoy ahead of him, he swam in the direction of the upturned lifeboat, stopping at intervals to shout, hoping to attract the attention of other survivors – if any existed. He received no answer and soon lost his bearings in the darkness. For another half-hour he swam around in circles, still calling. He was on the point of despair when he heard a faint answering shout. Nothing was visible, but the voice was real enough, calling out to guide him. Eventually he found the liferaft, whose sole occupant, twenty-one-year-old

Able Seaman Colin Armitage, was only too glad to help him on board.

For what remained of the night, Cooke and Armitage paddled their raft in a systematic search of the area, stopping from time to time to listen for voices. In this way they came upon Chief Steward Herbert Thornton, who gratefully joined them on their small wooden cockle-shell. Day was breaking when they found Chief Officer Basil Scown and, with great difficulty, hauled him on board. Scown, who had been in the water for three hours, had swallowed a great deal of oily water and was in bad shape.

The sun was well up when they sighted the second raft. It was empty but much larger than the one they were on, so they paddled towards it and transferred. Their new craft was of a much more substantial construction, and its tanks contained eight gallons of drinking-water and a number of tins of pemmican, Horlicks tablets and chocolate. The few provisions which had been in the smaller raft were brought on board, and the rafts were lashed together. With every hour that had passed since the sinking of the *Lulworth Hill*, Kenneth Cooke's luck had improved.

For the next few hours the four men laboriously paddled their rafts through the wreckage-strewn area, searching for more survivors. Their persistence was rewarded when they at last found the upturned lifeboat Cooke had seen in the beam of the submarine's searchlight. The six men astride its keel had been joined by four others, who were floating alongside them on a damaged liferaft.

The assorted craft of the tiny flotilla came together, and Chief Officer Scown, although he was very weak, took charge. His first action was to attempt to right the lifeboat, but the fourteen survivors were so near exhaustion that this proved impossible. Their task had not been made any easier by the appearance on the scene of a number of sharks, which circled menacingly around them.

It was finally decided to abandon both the lifeboat and the damaged raft. They distributed themselves on the two remaining rafts, ten men to the large one and four to the smaller. They were cramped but reasonably safe – for the time being. As to their future prospects, no one cared to voice an opinion, but they all had their thoughts.

A final search was then made among the wreckage for more survivors and for anything that might be of use to them. The result was disappointing. They netted only a single onion, which was found floating on the oil-covered water. By the time darkness came again, they knew they were all that remained of the *Lulworth Hill*'s crew of forty-six.

The fourteen survivors, six of them boys under eighteen settled down for the night, covering themselves with the small canvas sails found in the lockers of the rafts, but sleep proved impossible. The rafts were so crowded and the sea so rough that all their attention was directed to the struggle to avoid falling overboard. Scown was in a bad way, continally retching through the effects of the oil he had swallowed, and Second Engineer Eric Ledger, who had suffered injuries to both feet, was in constant pain. All fourteen were wet, covered in oil and thoroughly miserable.

After an hour or so of this torture, the men gave up all thoughts of sleep and huddled together discussing their chances of survival. Scown estimated that the *Lulworth Hill* had gone down in a position roughly 700 miles to the east of Angola and 900 miles south of the Gold Coast. In times of peace, the area would have been criss-crossed by dozens of ships on their way to and from the Cape of Good Hope. Now, with fewer ships at sea and many of those diverted well out into the Atlantic to avoid the U-boats, they were in the middle of nowhere, and the chance of rescue by a passing ship was not likely. An SSS message had been sent out at the time of the first attack on the night of the 18th, but the ship had gone down so fast when she was torpedoed next morning that there had been no opportunity to elaborate on it. It might be some days, perhaps weeks, before she was deemed overdue and the Royal Navy at Freetown set a search in motion.

Fortunately the weather in that part of the Atlantic is favourable throughout the year, with light to moderate south-easterly winds and a total absence of gales. On the other hand, rain rarely falls, and the cloudless skies give soaring temperatures during the day and cold nights to follow. The prevailing south-easterlies would be a help in enabling the rafts to make progress to the north, but the survivors' greatest adversary would be the South Equatorial Current, said to be one of the most constant currents in the world and, near the Equator, sets to the west at up to twenty miles a day. The rafts were in great danger of being swept out into mid-Atlantic.

It is probable that only Basil Scown, an experienced navigator, knew how heavily the odds were weighted against their survival. Had the others been aware, some would most certainly have given up hope. As it was, they were all prepared to make a try for the land to the north. With some difficulty, due to the overcrowding, the short masts of the rafts were stepped and the small square sails hoisted.

Accurate navigation of the cumbersome rafts, which had no rudders or compasses, was out of the question but, as so many resourceful seamen down the years had done before them, the survivors were confident they could keep their tiny craft pointing roughly in the right direction. At night the Southern Cross would always be there, shining brilliantly against a backdrop of black velvet, and could be kept astern. During the day, with only the sun circling overhead to guide them, it would be more difficult, but they would manage. As to which way the current was carrying them, they could only guess. When dawn came next day, look-outs were posted to scan the horizon for the help they still hoped might come – though how soon they dared not contemplate.

As day after day went by with the horizon remaining empty, morale declined rapidly. In daylight there was no shelter from the burning sun, and at night, no matter how close together they huddled, the cold bit cruelly into their bones. Fortunately the rafts were well stocked with the standard lifeboat rations of pemmican, Horlicks malted milk tablets, chocolate and hard biscuits, and the water tanks contained about thirty gallons. At first reckoning, it seemed they had ample food and water for survival. But for how long would they be adrift – days, weeks, months? Assuming the wind continued to blow from the south-east, Scown estimated they would make progress towards the land at about 1½ knots. They must then be prepared for an ordeal stretching to four or five weeks. The prospect was not inviting. Chief Steward Herbert Thornton had no illusions about his ability to survive more than thirty days, and he expressed his view to the others. Basil Scown, although cheerfully shouldering his responsibilities, was really seriously ill

from the effects of the oil he had swallowed. The condition of
Second Engineer Ledger was also deteriorating, as was that of
one of the young boys injured in the sinking.

Ten days later they were all still alive but dreadfully
emaciated, listless and covered with salt-water boils. Ledger and
the injured boy had both developed gangrene in their wounds,
and Scown was noticeably weaker. The sheer hopelessness of
their plight had mentally drained all of them, with the exception
of Cooke and Armitage, who seemed to possess some extra
quality that kept a tight grip on their minds. As Scown's
condition deteriorated, Cooke found himself gradually taking
over as leader of the pitiful little band.

On 6 April, when they had been eighteen days on the rafts,
Basil Scown lapsed into delirium and died. There were others in
the party who outranked the carpenter, but no objections were
raised when Cooke officially donned Scown's fallen mantle. His
greatest responsibility lay in keeping a watchful eye on the food
and water. Scown had set the daily ration per man at one ounce
of pemmican, one biscuit, four Horlicks tablets, three squares of
chocolate and six ounces of water. It was an insufficient,
monotonous and unpalatable diet, but Cooke had little choice
but to continue with it. The warm waters around them teemed
with fish, but without lines and hooks the survivors had no
means of availing themselves of that abundance of fresh food.
Cooke fashioned a crude harpoon from a marlin spike and a
length of driftwood but, while he was quite successful in
spearing fish, most of them slipped off the unbarbed spike
before they could be hauled on board. However, he did manage
to land the occasional salty morsel, which was devoured raw
with great relish.

As would be expected, the survivors' greatest enemy was
thirst – and it was not helped by the salty taste of the pemmican
and the sticky sweetness of the Horlicks tablets. Cooke caught
some of the young boys sipping salt water and took the firmest
action he could to stop the practice. During daylight he was able
to exercise strict control, but under the cover of darkness there
was little he could do.

Nothing could save Herbert Thornton, who, as he had
himself predicted, died on the thirtieth day. This was the
beginning of the end, for thereafter death was in daily

attendance on the rafts. Some died from the effects of drinking salt water; others were victims of the unremitting torture meted out by the elements, the merciless sun by day and the unrelenting cold at night. But in many cases it was lack of hope that killed. Physical fitness seemed to have little bearing on the sequence in which they died. Each time a man lost his faith in ultimate survival, he was doomed.

By 21 April, after thirty-three days, only Kenneth Cooke and Colin Armitage – ironically the original inhabitants of the rafts – remained alive. Both were strong-minded, resourceful individuals, and those characteristics undoubtedly helped them outlive the others. Caring for the weaker men, a role they had willingly assumed, had also left them little time to reflect on their own troubles.

When the last pathetic burial had taken place and Cooke and Armitage found themselves alone on the raft, they resolved that, having survived so far, they would make every effort to live to see the land again. Their first move was to cut loose the smaller, and now superfluous, raft, which was acting only as a drag on the larger one. Due solely to Cooke's careful husbandry over the preceding weeks, a good supply of food and water remained – certainly enough to last the two of them for many days to come.

The harvest from the sea also increased. With practice, Cooke had become quite efficient with his makeshift harpoon, and his daily haul was rising. The near-empty raft also proved fatally attractive to flying-fish, which flopped aboard, often three or four at a time. They were small, no bigger than sardines, but the two starving men consumed them with relish, leaving only the head and wings. Their new-found freedom of movement led to the discovery of a type of mussel growing in profusion just below the waterline of the raft. These shellfish were easily detached and proved a valuable source of food, part of the flesh containing a tiny sac of fresh water. Experimenting with a rope trailed behind the raft, they found this also quickly became covered with the small molluscs. Emboldened by their good fortune, they searched the sea around them for further sources of food and found strings of edible fish eggs. This warm-water caviar was a welcome addition to their main and monotonous diet of pemmican and malted milk tablets. As far as food and water were concerned, Cooke and Armitage were now well provided for, but their survival still hinged on the resilience of their minds.

As each dawn came and went and sea and sky remained stubbornly empty, the two men did their best not to give up hope, but their optimism eventually began to wear thin. They were now allowing themselves an increased basic diet – two ounces of pemmican, eight Horlicks tablets, five squares of chocolate and six ounces of water daily, but their physical condition was deteriorating. The presence of a great number of large sharks circling the raft did nothing to help their already tortured minds. Then, on 29 April, the forty-first day of their long trial, a flock of birds appeared overhead, and they knew they were at last nearing land. If they had had the strength to dance on the raft, Cooke and Armitage would have done so. As it was, a smile on their cracked lips was all they could muster.

At approximately 10.30 next morning, the last day of April, two aircraft flew directly over the raft, but at a great height. An excited Cooke set off two smoke flares, which sent up great orange clouds, but the aircraft gave no sign of having seen them and flew on out of sight. Disappointed though they were, the two survivors did not lose heart, for they were confident there would be other planes. When, in the middle of the afternoon, two more aircraft flew over – again without seeing their signal, their confidence was reinforced. They concluded they must be within the limits of the regular coastal patrols, originating in the Gold Coast or Sierra Leone.

The next day was one of bitter disappointment, for the sky was empty, except for a few circling sea-birds. Twenty-four hours later, on Sunday 2 May, two aircraft again flew over at a great height. Cooke set off another smoke float, but it produced no response. A few hours later, yet another aircraft was sighted, this time flying at a much lower altitude. It was for such an occasion that Cooke and Armitage had been saving their priceless stock of twelve red distress flares. They had no guarantee the flares would ignite, for they had been completely saturated when taken out of their so-called watertight tin during the early days on the raft. Each day they had been carefully placed in the sun to dry out, and each night they had equally carefully been stowed away. The testing time had now come.

The first flare failed to light, but the second erupted in a brilliant red flame and clouds of smoke which, lying low on the water, spread out over an area of almost two square miles. The effect was immediate. The aircraft first flew past the raft and then began to circle it, dropping lower with each circuit, its morse light flashing rapidly. Cooke and Armitage were too weak to make any pretence at reading the message of the light but they knew that, after forty-four days in which they had wandered the face of the ocean unseen, rescue was at last at hand. Tears ran down their salt-caked cheeks and they hugged each other unashamedly.

The plane now swooped low over the raft and dropped a number of packages into the sea. The two men had no strength left in their arms. Providentially two of the packages drifted close, and they were able to reach them with Cooke's harpoon. When opened, they were found to contain a rubber dinghy with a full set of stores, a kite and balloons complete with gas cylinders, a portable wireless transmitter, distress rockets and a Very pistol. The thing they needed most, fresh water, was not there, but they were so grateful for this long-awaited contact with the outside world that their thirst was forgotten. Night was approaching and, anticipating that morning would bring rescue, they lay down to rest. Due to their excited state, sleep largely eluded them, but that was of little consequence.

All through the following day they kept a keen look-out for ships and aircraft, but nothing came. Exhilaration turned to disappointment, and their sleep that night was again fitful. On the 4th they decided to set up the wireless transmitter. As their hands were stiff and awkward and the instruction book had been damaged by sea water, this proved to be a long task. The balloons would not inflate but, persevering, the two men succeeded in getting the kite into the air with the aerial attached. Neither had had any previous experience with a transmitter, but this set was designed for such a contingency. It was sufficient for them merely to crank the generator handles and tap out a series of SOSs with the morse key. They had no means of knowing if the set was actually transmitting but throughout the day, despite their weakened condition, they kept the generator going at the required speed and sent out a steady stream of distress calls.

Next morning it seemed that Christmas had come early. A Catalina flying-boat appeared and bombarded the sea around them with dozens of packages. Paddling the heavy raft was now completely beyond them, but they succeeded in inflating the rubber dinghy dropped by the first aircraft, and in this they picked up seven packages and brought them back to the raft. When opened, they were found to contain chocolate, barley sugar, chewing-gum, tins of various foods, cigarettes, matches, distress flares, a medical kit and, most welcome of all, tins of drinking-water. They also found a scribbled note from the airmen, which read:

> Sorry we can't get down to pick you up. Sea is too rough. Have sent signal from overhead for shore base to get a fix on you. Your signals are very clear and you have been heard in West Africa and Ascension Island. You are roughly 400 miles south of Liberia but in shipping lanes. Keep your chins up and keep smiling. Keep cracking away on transmitter, especially between hours of 11 a.m. and 2 p.m. (SOS, SOS and a continuous note). You should be picked up within 36 hours. If any shipping seen on way back to base, will direct them to you.

As they finished reading, the aircraft made a last run across the raft, dipped its wings and flew off to the north.

Cooke and Armitage felt that the death sentence which had been hanging over their heads for so long had been finally lifted. Stopping only to slake their thirst with the heaven-sent water, they went back to the transmitter with renewed enthusiasm, resting only when darkness fell.

With dawn next day they continued to transmit as they had been advised, and at 14.30 a large American flying-boat came in answer to their calls. The sea was still too rough for the pilot to attempt a landing, but more packages were dropped. Unfortunately they fell some miles from the raft and were wasted. The aircraft then flew away without making any effort to communicate with the survivors.

Four days had passed since they were first sighted from the air, but still the horizon remained empty of ships. Cooke and Armitage felt an air of hopelessness creeping over them. But throughout that day they persevered with their signals, which they now knew were being received. The night that followed was a bad one, for the sharks came back and spent much of the dark hours trying to overturn the raft.

By daybreak on the 7th, the two men were in desperate straits through fear and lack of sleep. Their despair deepened into near panic when the handles of the radio generator seized up and they were no longer able to call for help. It was as though an invisible umbilical chord connecting them to the world they so fervently wished to rejoin had been suddenly cut. Then, shortly before noon, as they were debating whether to risk opening up the transmitter in a bid to free the handles, Armitage glanced seaward and, to his amazement, saw the masts and funnel of a ship on the horizon.

Not daring to speak, in case the ship turned out to be some mirage-like product of their fevered imaginations, both men reached for the hand-held distress rockets they had received five days earlier. These proved to be spectacular, each rocket sending three brilliant balls of red fire high into the air. The first one fired, held by Armitage, resulted in a badly burnt hand; thereafter the men protected their hands with strips of wet canvas. Six rockets were launched, one after the other.

In spite of this impressive firework display, the ship did not alter course. In desperation, Cooke snatched up the Very pistol and sent flare after flare soaring skywards. This had the desired effect, for a warship now appeared on the scene and headed towards them. Determined not to go unnoticed, the survivors continued to fire rockets and flares until the warship was within a hundred yards of their raft. Half an hour later, the emaciated Cooke and Armitage were gently lifted aboard the destroyer HMS *Rapid*.

When they were rescued, on 7 May, Cooke and Armitage had been a little short of fifty days on the raft and had ended up 430 miles off the coast of Liberia, having covered a distance of 1,065 miles in a north-westerly direction. Much of their progress had been due to the South Equatorial Current, but it was the effect of the south-easterly wind acting on their small sail that had given them sufficient northing to edge the raft in towards the land and within range of the air patrols. Without the benefit of that scrap of canvas, they would have drifted into mid-Atlantic, there to meet a lonely end somewhere between the islands of Ascension and St Helena, where only the wheeling albatross and the patiently circling shark hold sway.

Cooke and Armitage were very near to death when picked up by the Royal Navy. Both men had lost almost forty-pounds in weight, and their hearts were so weak that the blood had all but ceased to circulate through their veins. For three weeks they were unable to walk unaided but, in the care of *Rapid*'s doctor and later in a Freetown hospital, they were eventually returned to full health. For their bravery and fortitude in the face of such terrible adversity, Kenneth Cooke and Colin Armitage were each awarded the George Medal. Armitage died in 1950, aged twenty-seven, a belated victim of that long voyage into the Gulf of Guinea.

As for the *Leonardo da Vinci*, she was to do little more damage to the Allied cause, sinking only one more ship before being caught by the British destroyers *Active* and *Ness* off the Azores and sent to the bottom on 23 may 1943. Ironically it was on that very day that Cooke and Armitage were landed by HMS *Rapid* in Freetown.

13   Mediterranean Nightmare

The chill of the short Mediterranean winter was still in the air when, soon after dawn on 13 March 1943, the British cargo ship *Ocean Voyager* left the bustle of Alexandria harbour astern and set course to the westwards. The sky was clear but a freshening north-westerly wind was busy herding white horses across a steel-grey sea to run headlong into the bluff bows of the ship as she worked up to full speed.

After the smell and dust of Alexandria, the crisp morning air was like wine to Captain Duncan Mackellar as he paced the bridge of the *Ocean Voyager* mulling over the likely problems of the passage ahead. Steaming at her top speed of eleven knots, it would take the ship just over 3½ days to reach her destination, the Libyan port of Tripoli, which lay 950 miles to the west. In earlier years, when peace reigned over that pleasant sea, Mackellar would have welcomed the relief afforded by the short passage through open and untroubled waters. For him, it would have been a temporary escape from all the commercial and political pressures which burden a shipmaster in a foreign port, a time to step back and allow his officers to run the ship. Unfortunately in the spring of 1943 the Mediterranean was not a place to drop one's guard, for the enemy was in a spiteful mood.

The Germans' reaction to the plight of the Afrika Corps, fleeing before the hammer-blows of Montgomery's Eighth Army, had been to concentrate their ire on the thinly stretched British supply line, the merchant ships running a shuttle-service with stores and ammunition from Alexandria to Benghazi and Tripoli. To that end, Admiral Dönitz had in the Mediterranean under his command twenty-three German and a dozen or so Italian U-boats. For them, the *Ocean Voyager*, loaded with 2,500 tons of high explosives, 3,000 tons of aviation spirit and 1,000 tons of military stores, sailing unescorted at the speed of a horse-drawn carriage, presented a primary and highly vulnerable target.

Built in 1942 at the Todd Yard in California, the 7,174-ton *Ocean Voyager* was one of a breed of wartime, mass-produced, prefabricated vessels. At a time when U-boats were sinking Allied merchant vessels faster than they could normally be built, the American yards were fortunately turning these ships out at fifty-day intervals. The *Ocean Voyager* was, in consequence, even more basic than the average tramp of earlier years, having a barge-shaped hull and a triple-expansion steam-engine a size too small for her 7,000 tons. Her crew accommodation was so basic that it missed contravening the Merchant Shipping Act of 1894 by a hair's breadth. Owned by the Ministry of War Transport, she was managed by H. Hogarth & Sons of Glasgow, one of the largest privately owned tramp fleets in the world, whose roots went back to 1868.

In her favour, the *Ocean Voyager* was strongly built, and her crew of forty-four mainly Scottish, were typcial of the men who ran Britain's tramp ships: intelligent, resourceful and tenacious. Her armament consisted of an American-made three-inch gun mounted aft, four 20 mm Oerlikons, two twin Marlin, two Army Colt and two Lewis machine-guns. These guns were manned by nine DEMS gunners, drawn from the Royal Navy and the Maritime Anti-Aircraft Regiment. For the passage to Tripoli, she also carried two military policemen, whose role was to guard the 3,000 bags of Army mail on board.

Having successfully run the gauntlet of the U-boats, the *Ocean Voyager* arrived off Tripoli in the late afternoon of 16 March. The port, which had spent much of its time in slumber since it was founded by the Phoenicians, was humming like a disturbed beehive, with all berths occupied by a motley fleet of cargo ships discharging weapons and stores for the advancing British troops. It was at first thought that the *Ocean Voyager* would have to wait outside the port, but an anchorage was eventually found for her inside the breakwaters, cheek by jowl with a throng of tankers, ammunition ships and naval vessels.

As he looked around the forest of masts and derricks cramming the port, Captain Mackellar could not suppress a feeling of unease. He was not happy with the way his ship was hemmed in. Since Tripoli had been reopened in early February, it had been the target of frequent and determined attacks by Axis bombers. In the event of such an attack occurring within the next few days, the *Ocean Voyager*, with her lethal mixture of ammunition and high octane below decks, would be trapped like a hobbled horse in a burning stable. If that time came, he hoped he and his men would be equal to the situation.

The first night passed without incident, and on the morning of the 17th barges were placed alongside the *Ocean Voyager* for the off-loading of her vital cargo. All local shore labour had long since taken to the hills, and Mackellar was faced with the unenviable task of having to order his crew to discharge their own cargo. As in the case of all British merchant ships, there was a clause in the Articles of Agreement, signed by both officers and ratings of the *Ocean Voyager*, which called upon them to work cargo in port as and when required by the master. Under normal circumstances, it is a poor shipmaster who will attempt to heap this additional burden on his crew without good cause. In this case, the *Ocean Voyager*'s officers and ratings to a man agreed to work the ship without argument. Their philosophy was typical of the British merchant seamen of the day, preferring to get on with the job, rather than debate the merits of the case. There would be time for that later.

Under the supervision of Chief Officer George Stronach, derricks were rigged, winches manned and, with officer and rating working side by side, the discharging commenced. By late afternoon on the 19th, some 1,700 tons had been off-loaded onto the barges, a creditable performance, given the circumstances. Stronach had planned to work until dark that day, but heavy rain began to fall at 17.00 and he was forced to call a halt. Having worked almost non-stop since 06.00 that morning, the men were tired and dirty, and there were no protests when Stronach ordered them below to wash and rest. He considered leaving a watch on deck to look out for enemy aircraft but decided against it as it seemed an unfair burden on those chosen for duty. The port had been free from attack for several days and it seemed reasonable to take a risk – just for that night. In any case, he had been advised by the shore authorities that the air-raid alarm would be sounded at least fifteen minutes before any raiders arrived over the port. That would give his men ample time to get to their action stations.

At that time, George Stronach and those ashore were unaware of two crucial developments. High above the clouds, 200 miles to the north, a force of twelve JU-88 bombers, groaning under a load of bombs, torpedoes and parachute mines, was winging its way towards Tripoli. Meanwhile, saboteurs in the port had succeeded in cutting the wires to the air-raid sirens.

Forty-five minutes later, Stronach, having bathed and eaten a good meal, was half-dozing in his cabin when the banging of anti-aircraft batteries ashore brought him abruptly awake. He reached the lower bridge as the bombs came raining down out of the low-hanging clouds. The *Ocean Voyager* was hit three times in as many minutes, one bomb crashing into her No.2 hatch, while two others hit her bridge front. Stronach was knocked off his feet by the blast and lost consciousness. As he fell to the deck, a fourth bomb exploded in No.5 hold.

Second Engineer Hezikiah Hotham, a fifty-eight-year-old Humberside man, was on watch in the engine-room when the *Ocean Voyager* reeled under under the blast of the bomb salvo. The lights went out and Hotham was left deafened, cursing and fumbling for his torch. With the firemen of his watch racing up the ladders ahead of him, he reached the deck to find the ship on fire fore and aft. Moving forward to investigate, he found the bridge accommodation completely wrecked and blazing furiously. The upper part of the bridge appeared to have collapsed into No.2 hold, and flames were leaping from the hatchway. Hotham recalled the neat rows of 250-pound bombs he had seen resting on cases of high octane in the hold and, despite the heat around him, broke out in a cold sweat. His instinct for survival urged him to make for the ship's side rail and throw himself into the harbour before the ship blew herself apart. But that unexplainable loyalty every seaman feels for his ship, no matter how imperfect she be, asserted itself and he looked around for help. There was a chance the fires could be fought and extinguished before the cataclysm came.

Luckily for George Stronach, the blast from the bombs that destroyed the bridge had thrown him underneath one of the lifeboats, where he had been sheltered from falling debris. When he regained consciousness, his body ached from multiple burns and bruises, one eye was closed and his uniform was in tatters, but he appeared to have escaped serious injury. He got unsteadily to his feet and set out to explore the holocaust which was once his ship.

As Hotham had already discovered, the bridge house was a blazing inferno, part of it having fallen into No.2 hold. The cargo in the hold was on fire, with the crack of exploding small arms ammunition adding to the roar of the flames. In the rigging abreast the hatch, the wreckage of a German bomber which had crashed into the ship was still smouldering. Further forward, Stronach could see clouds of dense white smoke pouring from No.1 hold, while abaft the bridge No.3 hold was also belching smoke and flames.

The situation was as bad as it could possibly be, but Stronach was a Glasgow man and not in the habit of stepping aside from trouble. Picking his way through the wreckage, he made his way down to the main deck, where he met up with Second Engineer Hotham. No other crew members were to be seen, and the two officers decided that the loss of life caused by the enemy bombs must have been catastrophic. However, they were of one mind as to what should be done. Although he was putting his life in great danger, Hotham volunteered to return to the deserted engine-room to speed up the deck water-pumps. Stronach then went forward to No.2 hatch and coupled up a firehose, with the intention of playing water on the fire in the hold. His efforts were wasted, for the deck service line had been fractured and only a trickle came out of the nozzle of the hose. The flames from the hatchway were now shooting forty feet in the air, and the *Ocean Voyager*'s predicament was too awful to contemplate. It must be only a matter of time – minutes, perhaps – before the bombs in her No.2 hold were set off by the heat.

At that critical point Stronach was relieved to see his senior petty officer, Boatswain Gardiner, appear on the scene. Like many others, Gardiner had been resting in his cabin after the day's work when the bombs fell. Pausing only to grip the boatswain's arm in encouragement, Stronach sent him below to help Hotham. If they were to stand any chance of saving the ship, they must have more pressure on the fire hydrants.

When Gardiner had gone below, Stronach threw down his

useless hose and made his way quickly aft to No.3 hatch, where the ship's foam-generating equipment was stowed. His journey was in vain, for he discovered the equipment had been smashed by the blast. Even to the tenacious Glaswegian, the situation now looked hopeless. The aviation spirit was well alight in all holds, and the rumble of exploding drums ran the length of the ship. Flames roared and crackled, accompanied by the crash of exploding shells, grenades and bullets. It was Dante's *Inferno* re-enacted, and Stronach decided it was high time to evacuate any of those who might still be alive. He began a search of the ship.

Right aft, in the crew's forecastle, he came upon sixteen of the ship's older ratings sheltering in the alleyway. Many of them were bleeding from splinter wounds, and they were all very frightened. Stronach had great difficulty in persuading them to follow him on deck but eventually led them to No.4 hatch, where the motor lifeboat, which had been used for communication with the shore, was still tied up alongside. At that moment Gardiner re-appeared from the engine-room, and Stronach put him in charge of the boat, instructing him to take the men to the nearest naval ship for medical attention.

Having satisfied himself that the boatswain had the evacuation of the wounded men in hand, Stronach made his way back to the boat-deck, intending to lower the port lifeboat and secure it alongside ready to take any other survivors he might find. He would need to work swiftly, for he sensed that the ship might soon be on the point of exploding.

As the *Ocean Voyager*'s lifeboat davits were of the geared quadrant type, Stronach was able to swing the boat out and lower it to the water single-handed. It was only when he had completed the task that he realized he was not alone on the boat-deck. On the raised gun-platform on the port side, DEMS Gunner R. Rutherford was still at his post, manning the Oerlikon and scanning the night sky for enemy planes. Either oblivious to or contemptuous of the falling bombs, Rutherford had been at his gun from the start of the attack and was probably responsible for the destruction of the enemy plane which crashed into the *Ocean Voyager*'s rigging. He had no intention of deserting the ship and waved aside Stronach's invitation to take to the boat.

Stronach descended to the main deck and went back amidships, continuing his search for survivors. The heat from the leaping flames was searing his bare skin, and he stopped abreast No.3 hatch to soak his remaining rags of clothes and his body with a trickle of water from a fire hose. Then he made a run for the bridge accommodation.

The whole of the bridge house seemed now to have collapsed on itself, and for a brief moment Stronach hesitated. There could surely be no one alive in the tangled, smoking ruin which had once housed the *Ocean Voyager*'s deck officers. But he went on and, after several attempts, forced his way into the officer's bathroom, where he found Second Officer C. Morris lying on the deck unconscious. Morris, who had obviously been taking a bath when the bombs fell, was naked, his face was covered in blood and he had serious burns. Stronach feared the man was dead, but he found a pulse and then dragged Morris clear of the wreckage and out onto the deck. By that time the second officer had recovered consciousness and was able to gasp out to Stronach that other men were trapped inside the accommodation. Without hesitation, Stronach went back.

Flames from the inferno in No.2 hold were now threatening to engulf the blackened shell of the bridge house, and Stronach, courageous though he was, realized it would serve no useful purpose to throw away his own life by entering the accommodation again. Then he heard faint groans coming from the outboard alleyway on the port side and clawed his way through the fallen debris until he found Chief Engineer James Anderson trapped half in and half out of a cabin porthole. Anderson, who was in terrible agony, explained that the bulkheads of the cabin had fallen, breaking both his legs. While he was attempting to escape through the porthole, the heavy steel deadlight had fallen on his back and he could not move.

The Chief was a big man, and Stronach, choking on the black smoke and seared by the flames leaping around him, had great difficulty in extricating him. Somehow – he never did quite understand how he had succeeded – he levered up the heavy deadlight, prised the groaning Anderson out of the porthole and lowered him none too gently to the deck. He then dragged the injured man aft to No.3 hatch, where he had left the semi-conscious Morris. He tied a rope around the Chief's waist and prepared to lower him into the lifeboat lying alongside. But Stronach's own strength was now failing, and he was unable to lift Anderson over the rail.

Rutherford, who was still manning the Oerlikon and firing whenever an enemy plane came within his sights, saw Stronach's obvious difficulty and jumped down from his post to lend a hand. At the same time Hotham appeared on deck, and between them the three men lowered Anderson and Morris into the waiting lifeboat. Stronach then ordered Rutherford to take the boat and the injured men to safety.

By now, the situation in the harbour was almost as bad as that on board the burning *Ocean Voyager*. The bombs were still falling, and a small Greek tanker anchored nearby had been sunk and was spewing blazing petrol onto the water. Into this roaring furnace three German bombers then crashed, adding to the horror of the night. Much of the surface of the water in the harbour was ablaze, and the flames were drifting purposefully towards the *Ocean Voyager*, herself already a burning torch.

While Stronach had been engaged in his gallant rescue attempt on board, Gardiner had been faced with the unenviable task of taking his lifeboat and its sixteen injured and frightened passengers away from the ship. He had been unable to find the key to start the boat's engine, and it was proving difficult to calm the men and persuade them to ship the oars. This he eventually did – assisted, no doubt, by the fire raging on three sides. The men at first wanted to row to an American ship, which had so far escaped unharmed in the bombing, but Gardiner knew that that ship was also loaded with ammunition and had no intention of boarding such a vulnerable refuge. After some argument, Gardiner put his stamp of authority on the men, and they rowed in some semblance of unison towards a British destroyer, which took them on board. The wounded were given medical attention, and hot drinks and dry clothing appeared as if by magic.

But the survivors' night of agony was not yet over. Half and hour after their rescue, the destroyer was struck by an aerial torpedo and began to sink. Fortunately there were now plenty of small craft at hand, and the *Ocean Voyager*'s men were taken off and landed ashore.

Back aboard the blazing ship, Stronach and Hotham

continued their search for survivors. They were particularly concerned for Captain Mackellar, who had not been seen since the first bombs fell. Returning amidships, they made determined efforts to penetrate the bridge accommodation but were forced back by debris, flames and smoke. The finally agreed that, if Mackellar was lying somewhere under the wreckage, he either was dead or would die soon, for there was no way to reach him.

There was now no good reason why Stronach and Hotham should not take steps to safeguard their own lives, but they were stubborn men and still had their minds set on saving the ship. Hotham volunteered to return to the engine-room in the hope that he might be able to increase the pressure on the deck service water.

While he awaited developments, Stronach carried on looking for the living and the dead. It was the dead he found first. In the orange light of the dancing flames he came across the body of Captain Duncan Mackellar lying on the port side of the deck. Mackellar's injuries were extensive, and he had without doubt been killed outright by the exploding bombs. There was nothing Stronach could do for him but to say a silent goodbye.

Crossing to the starboard side of the deck, Stronach continued the search and found Third Radio Officer M. Frankland lying in the scuppers. A quick examination showed Frankland to have severe head injuries and a broken leg, but he was still alive. Stronach slipped his arms under the wounded man's shoulders and dragged him aft towards a liferaft, which he believed was the only item of life-saving equipment left on board. The raft was already in the water and being paddled away from the ship by two late survivors, but in response to Stronach's shouts the men brought the raft back alongside and Frankland was put aboard.

At Stronach's back, the fire in No.3 hold had reached a spectacular peak, with smoke and flames billowing from the hatchway, accompanied by the crack of exploding ammunition below. The bulkheads were glowing white-hot, and as that hold contained a quantity of thousand-pound bombs, Stronach reluctantly decided it was time to go. He went to the top of the engine-room and called to Hotham to come up.

Before finally abandoning the ship, Stronach made one last

round of the decks. His persistence was rewarded when he stumbled over Greaser O'Shay, who was lying unconscious on the starboard side of the after deck. O'Shay was badly burned but still living. When Hotham arrived, the two men carried the greaser to the ship's side, only to find that the liferaft had drifted away. The *Ocean Voyager* was now ablaze from stem to stern, and time was running out for the three men left alive on board. Stronach and Hotham hurriedly forced a lifejacket onto the unconscious O'Shay and unceremoniously threw him overboard. It was the only way they could give the greaser a chance to live.

Stronach then dived into the sea and swam towards the drifting raft. When he clambered aboard, he found that the two thoroughly demoralized occupants had lost their paddles. He wasted no time in commiseration and bullied the men into paddling with their hands towards a burning lighter. Stronach was aware that the lighter had on board ammunition discharged from the *Ocean Voyager* earlier in the day and was itself in danger of blowing up, but he desperately needed a means of propelling the raft, and the planks of dunnage wood on the decks of the lighter were all there was on offer. He put the raft alongside, boarded the lighter and, despite the heat and flames, rummaged around until he found pieces of wood suitable for use as paddles. The raft then returned to the ship, where Second Engineer Hotham was taken off and O'Shay pulled out of the water.

The burning oil on the waters of the harbour was now closing in around them, and smoking debris rained down on their heads from the erupting holds of the *Ocean Voyager*. Fear lent strength to their muscles, and they paddled clear of the oncoming flames and out into the darkness of a smoke-screen which had been laid across the harbour to confuse the bombers. For the next half hour they wandered aimlessly through the oily, evil-smelling fog, uncertain in which direction safety lay. The indomitable Stronach used his whistle to signal for help, and at last a naval launch, which had been patrolling the perimeter of the burning oil, came to their rescue. The six men were put ashore at 20.30, the injured rushed to hospital and Stronach, Hotham and the two others accommodated at the Merchant Navy Club, about one mile from the harbour.

It would seem that, for George Stronach and Hezikiah Hotham, the long Mediterranean nightmare was over and they would now be rewarded with the sleep of the just. But the *Ocean Voyager* had not finished with those who had tried so hard to save her. A little before midnight, she blew herself apart with an explosion so great that the blast partly demolished the Merchant Navy Club. Stronach and Hotham were jerked rudely out of their sleep of exhaustion and spent the next few hours digging out one of the *Ocean Voyager*'s firemen, who had been trapped by a falling wall.

When daylight came, there was little to be seen of the *Ocean Voyager*. Parts of her bow and stern lay half-submerged alongside the quay, but most of her had been scattered in ragged sections all over the town and harbour. One of her boilers, crushed like a huge tin can, was found more than two miles from the wreck. A number of ships in the harbour had suffered damage from flying debris.

The reckoning in human terms of the bombing of the *Ocean Voyager* made grim reading. Captain Duncan Mackellar had been killed outright and Greaser O'Shay later died of his burns. Four men, Third Officer Norman Wright, First Radio Officer Samuel Smyth, Chief Steward Percy Appleton and a military policeman were missing, and twelve others were injured. Undoubtedly, had it not been for the combined efforts of Chief Officer George Stronach, Second Engineer Hezikiah Hotham, Boatswain Gardiner and Gunner R. Rutherford, many more would have lost their lives. George Stronach, burned and bruised and with a splinter in one eye which rendered him partially blind, had throughout shown magnificent leadership and stubborn courage in the finest Nelsonian tradition. Hotham was to say of him: 'I would like to place on record a tribute to Chief Officer G.P. Stronach, who throughout displayed exceptional courage in remaining on board to rescue so many survivors, who undoubtedly would otherwise have lost their lives. His cool bravery in the face of overwhelming odds was outstanding, and throughout he was under the impression that he was doing nothing more than his duty. Despite the almost incredible feats which he performed, his only fear was that he had perhaps not done enough.' Boatswain Gardiner had this to offer on the subject: 'There is no doubt at all that Chief Officer

Stronach displayed incredible heroism in remaining on this blazing inferno for such a long time, fully knowing that the ship was likely to blow up at any minute. Many of the ship's personnel owe their lives to his cool courage, fortitude and complete disregard for his own personal safety.'

Hezikiah Hotham, although he was nearing his sixtieth year, on that awful night showed the bulldog-like determination and casual bravery that have been characteristic of British Merchant Navy engineers for generations. George Stronach put on record: 'Although aged fifty-eight, this officer displayed magnificent courage and initiative such as is not generally found, even in younger men. Without his untiring help, it would have been physcially impossible to have rescued any survivors. I consider his gallant action in going into the engine-room and staying there to attend to the pumps was truly magnificent, as he was fully aware of the many and extreme dangers, including that of a major explosion, which might have occurred at any moment.' Stronach's praise of Gunner Rutherford was no less generous: 'The gallantry and cool bearing of DEMS Gunner R. Rutherford were also magnificent and inspiring. After all the younger members of the crew had jumped overboard, he went to his gun and continued to repel the attack completely unaided. His unselfish action and complete disregard for his own personal safety were a wonderful example to all and were in accordance with the highest traditions of the Service to which he belongs.'

The *Ocean Voyager* was barely a year off the slipway when that catastrophic explosion ripped her apart in Tripoli harbour on the night of 19 March 1943, but she and her men did not die in vain. Other ships followed close in her wake, loaded to their marks with sufficient ammunition and supplies for Montgomery's army to keep up the momentum of its advance.

On 12 May, having been driven into the Cape Bon peninsula with their backs to the sea, 250,415 German and Italian trooops laid down their arms. The final battle of the Western Desert had been won.

14   Appointment off Minicoy

In early September 1943 the Indian Ocean, sometime haunt of Henry Every, William Kidd and a host of their piratical contemporaries, was once more a sea bristling with dangers for the lone merchantman. Throughout the preceding months of the year, a wide-ranging force of enemy submarines, estimated to be seven German and eight Japanese, had reaped a rich harvest amongst those whose paths crossed that lonely sea. Of the increased number of Allied ships bringing supplies to India for the planned re-entry into Burma by Lord Louis Mountbatten's forces, at least fifty-seven totalling 337,169 tons, had been sent to the bottom. The Royal Navy, which had kept the peace in that ocean for centuries past, was strenuously occupied elsewhere and could spare only a handful of old cruisers and armed merchantmen for convoy escort duty. It was inevitable that many merchant ships were, therefore, left to fend for themselves in those waters. One such unfortunate was the 5,150-ton *Larchbank*.

Owned by Andrew Weir & Company of London and built on the Clyde in 1925 by Harland & Wolf, the *Larchbank* was a solidly built, twin-screw motorship, designed for extended voyages and therefore geared to self-sufficiency. In her younger days she had managed a steady twelve knots, but age and the rigours of the trade had long reduced her to a laborious plod that rarely exceeded ten knots. Under the command of Captain William McCracken, she was crewed by nineteen British officers and forty Lascar seamen. Added to her normal complement by the exigencies of war were ten DEMS gunners, two Royal Navy petty officers on special assignment and five Lascar seamen taking passage back to India following the loss of their own ship. This gave her a total complement for the voyage of seventy-six.

The *Larchbank* had loaded in the American east-coast port of Baltimore for Calcutta and had on board several thousand tons of railway iron, four tanks, two amphibian trucks, various military stores and, on deck, two motor torpedo boats, which were in the care of the two RN petty officers.

Thirty days out of Baltimore, the *Larchbank* left Aden on 1 September, bound for Colombo, Ceylon, where she would bunker before continuing her voyage to Calcutta. Her route lay across the Gulf of Aden to a position close north of the forbidding island of Socotra, thence through the seventy-mile-wide channel between the Laccadive and Maldive Islands, and so south-east to Colombo. With the South-West Monsoon still blowing, the weather for much of the 2,000-mile passage was likely to be anything but favourable. As soon as the *Larchbank* drew clear of the Horn of Africa, she would be beam on to the strong south-westerly winds and rough seas generated by the deep summer depression over North India. A predominantly overcast sky, with frequent heavy rain squalls, would give little opportunity for use of the sextant, reducing navigation to the realms of educated guesswork. At that season, even in times of peace, the passage was never an enjoyable one; with German and Japanese submarines known to be active in the area, it appeared less attractive still. Making, at the best, ten knots, the *Larchbank* would be extremely vulnerable throughout. Granted, she was well armed, mounting a four-inch, a twelve-pounder and five 20 mm Oerlikons, crewed by ten experienced DEMS gunners but, as William McCracken well knew, all this considerable firepower would amount to naught against a submerged submarine.

One thousand miles to the east, deep in the Arabian Sea, the Japanese submarine *I-27* cruised hopefully under a grey, rain-laden sky. In the conning-tower, her commander, Toshiaki Fukumura, gripped the handrail and sucked at his teeth nervously as the trimmed-down boat buried her bows in yet another huge comber and rose again, streaming water like a half-tide rock. The strain of the long patrol was beginning to show on Fukumura's normally impassive face. His boat was short of fuel and provisions, and ominous cracks were appearing in the morale of his well-disciplined crew. Since the sinking of the 6,797-ton American Freighter *Alcoa Prospector* in the Gulf of

Oman two months previously, the horizon had remained empty of suitable targets. Fukumura was reaching the point where he would gladly have wasted one of his precious torpedoes on a down-at-heel Arab dhow in the interest of breaking the awful monotony. Yet, such was his luck, he had not even flushed out as much as a fishing canoe.

On the evening of Thursday 9 September, the *Larchbank* was in the vicinity of Minicoy Island, a low, sandy atoll which forms the northern marker of the Eight Degree Channel, one of the deep-water routes through the Maldives. She was just over 400 miles from Colombo, having crossed the Arabian Sea without molestation.

Soon after 20.00, Second Engineer Pain and Junior Fourth Engineer Goodall emerged from the engine-room with their white boilersuits grimy and soaked in sweat. The four-hour watch they had just completed below in a temperature in excess of 100°F had been the equivalent of a sustained Turkish bath. Stopping only to pick up two cups of tea and a plate of sandwiches at the pantry, the two men moved out onto the after deck, grateful for the touch of the cool evening air on their clammy bodies. It was a fine, clear night, with – for the first time since leaving Aden – the heavy clouds having cleared away to reveal the tropical night sky studded with a myriad diamond-chip stars.

Pain and Goodall settled themselves side by side on the tarpaulin-covered hatch-top to watch the new moon rise, sipping warily at the hot, strong tea and biting with relish into the cold beef sandwiches. No words passed between them, but their thoughts were in tune. It was at a time like that that all the hardship and discomfort involved in life at sea seemed suddenly worth while. No man safe on shore could ever experience such blessed peace and contentment at the end of a day's work.

The silver crescent moon was only a hand's breadth above the horizon when the two watchkeepers were joined by Captain McCracken and his chief engineer, James Ford, who were also sampling the night air. For ten minutes or so the four men chatted amiably, the main topic of conversation being the shore-going attractions offered by the port of Colombo, where McCracken estimated they would arrive at noon on Saturday. On this occasion, the engineers would be fully occupied taking bunkers during the short stay in port, but they had memories enough of Mount Lavinia, the Galle Face Hotel and other less salubrious haunts. Colombo was a good place for a run ashore.

At about 20.30 the little group split up, McCracken and Ford to continue their walk, Pain and Goodall going to their respective cabins. After a quick shower in tepid water, thirty-four-year-old Douglas Goodall turned in on top of his bunk, wearing only a pair of shorts, for the heat in his tiny cabin was only marginally less than in the engine-room, over which it was situated. Before dropping off into an uneasy sleep, Goodall's thoughts turned to his wife Elizabeth and their small house overlooking the Firth of Forth. Drowsily, he wondered if the soft rain was falling there now, as it had been on the day he left. Or was the sun shining down out of a clear autumn sky, turning the normally steel-grey waters of the Forth to an inviting blue? It had been that way when they first met. How many more months would pass before he saw Elizabeth and Scotland again?

Out in the darkness of the night, on the *Larchbank*'s port side, the ghostly shape of *I-27* slid through the water unseen, as Toshiaki Fukumura continued his remorseless search for another victim. Fukumura's long-standing frustration had not been eased by a disastrous encounter with an American merchantman, the 7,176-ton *Lyman Stewart*, forty-eight hours earlier. Of the five torpedoes fired at the freighter, only one had hit – and that proved to be a dud. Fukumura had then surfaced and opened fire with his deck gun but could inflict only minor damage on the ship. He had caught up with the wily American again in the early hours of that morning, but once more his attack had failed miserably. The *Lyman Stewart* had gone on her way unharmed, leaving Fukumura and his crew suffering severe loss of face. The Japanese commander was determined this would not happen again.

On the bridge of the *Larchbank*, Third Officer Buchan, officer of the watch, paced the port wing, stopping from time to time to sweep the dark line of the horizon with his binoculars. The night was quiet, disturbed only by the muted thump of the ship's two six-cylinder diesels and the creaking of her derricks in their crutches as she rolled in the heavy swell. The standby quartermaster moved into the shadows of the wheel-house to strike four bells, indicating the halfway point of the watch.

Having listened to the bells repeated by the look-out man on the forecastle head, Buchan decided it was also time to break the monotony of the watch with a cup of tea. He took a last look around the horizon preparatory to visiting the chart-room – and suddenly froze. Crossing the ship's bow close ahead, moving swiftly from port to starboard, he saw a long trail of bubbling phosphorescence. It might have been only the track of a cruising porpoise, but Buchan was not prepared to speculate – which was just as well, for as he lunged for the alarm-bell switch, a second line of bubbles came racing in towards the *Larchbank*'s port beam. This time Fukumura's torpedo did not fail to explode.

Douglas Goodall awoke from his fitful sleep with the crash of the exploding torpedo ringing in his ears. He shot upright in his bunk, dazed and wondering if he was caught up in one of those horrendous nightmares that so often haunted those who lived and slept cheek by jowl with violent death in that awful war. Then the ship shuddered violently, and the air was filled with the stench of burning oil. Goodall realized that this was no nightmare, but stark reality.

He rolled clear of his bunk and, with an instinctive reaction the romantics would make much of, reached for his wife's photograph, which stood on the chest of drawers alongside the bunk. As he did so, the ship lurched heavily to starboard, and the photograph slid off the polished top of the chest to fall with a splintering of glass on the deck. Realizing he had no time to waste if he were to save his life, Goodall struggled into his lifejacket, falling against the bulkhead and then out into the alleyway as the *Larchbank* gave another lurch.

The alleyway was awash but the lights were still on, and Goodall was relieved to find himself in the company of Chief Engineer Ford and the two engineers of the 8-12 watch, who had just evacuated the engine-room. Having ascertained from the watchkeepers that the ship had been torpedoed on the port side in the way of No.4 and No.5 holds, Ford led the way on deck. As they passed the engine-room door, he paused to pull the emergency stops of the main engine fuel-valves. Following Ford and the others out on deck, Goodall tripped over the bodies of two officers, but he could not stop to identify them.

The after deck of the *Larchbank* resembled a battlefield.

Derricks were broken and bent, and the holds had been stripped of their hatchboards and tarpaulins. The motor torpedo boat which had been stowed on No.4 hatch-top was hanging drunkenly over the side, secured only by a few frayed wire lashings. A red glow emanated from the open holds, and the ominous crackling of flames came from below. The plates of the main deck were awash with cascading, foaming water.

The four engineers scrambled up the ladder to the boat-deck, where they separated, the watchkeepers going to their station on the starboard side, and Ford and Goodall to the forward port lifeboat. There they found the deck serang and one of the sailors in the act of lowering the boat, which was fully manned. Ford ordered the two Indians into the boat, and he and Goddall took over the falls.

The boat was safely lowered to the water but, owing to the large swell running, its occupants were unable to release the after block. As they struggled, the boat lifted on the swell until it was level with the boat-deck and, when the sea subsided, was left hanging bow-down, suspended by the after fall. Ford and Goodall watched helpless as the Indians fought in vain to clear the jammed block. The next swell smashed the lifeboat against the ship's side, breaking it in two and spilling the screaming men into the dark, angry water alongside.

Horror-stricken, the two engineers raced to the after end of the deck and made ready to jump over the side, for it was clear the *Larchbank* would not survive many more minutes. They stood at the rail, hesitating, for neither man could swim. Then the decision was made for them when a wall of green water slammed against the ship's side and surged upwards, sweeping them off their feet.

Goodall ended up in the starboard scuppers and, before he could regain his feet, the *Larchbank* gave a slow roll and slid beneath the waves, taking him with her.

Fortunately Goodall did not panic but held his breath as he went down and down into gloomy depths, drawn by the powerful suction of the sinking ship. He had always scoffed at tales of dying men seeing the events of their lives flash before their eyes, but that was exactly what he experienced now. At last, when his lungs were on the point of bursting, the *Larchbank* released her hold and he shot to the surface. Luckily he surfaced close to a packing-case, which he clung to while he regained his breath. The sea around him was covered in floating wreckage, and where the *Larchbank* had been, there remained above the water only her fore-topmast, on which a red light still burned eerily. Then that too was gone.

The new moon was now high in the sky and casting a good light, by which Goodall saw a small wooden liferaft bobbing on the waves twenty yards away. Being unable to swim, he was reluctant to relinquish his hold on the packing-case, but the raft beckoned temptingly. After hesitating for a minute or so, he kicked clear and paddled laboriously across the intervening stretch of water, thanking God for his lifejacket. When he reached the raft and dragged himself aboard, he was exhausted. But he had little time to dwell on his physical state, for he heard shouts close by. He was soon helping aboard the raft the *Larchbank*'s engine-room serang and one of her sailors.

For the next hour, the three men lay side by side on the heaving raft, miserable but thankful to be alive. Then the sound of paddles was heard and a larger liferaft came into sight. On board were Third Radio Officer J. Glendenning, Chief Motor Mechanic John Ives, one of the POs in charge of the MTBs, an apprentice and two Lascar seamen. It was decided to lash the two rafts together, and they lay drifting side by side to await the coming of daylight.

With dawn on the 10th came a strong south-westerly wind, which quickly whipped up an angry sea. By 08.00, it had become so rough that the rope joining the two rafts snapped and they drifted apart. Douglas Goodall and his two companions were alone again.

Noon brought fresh hope. One of the *Larchbank*'s lifeboats, containing Chief Engineer Ford and twenty-three other men, appeared on the scene. Ford, who had spent two hours in the water after the ship sank, brought the boat alongside Goodall's raft, and they were later joined by the larger liferaft. Assembled, it would seem, were the only survivors of the sinking of the *Larchbank*, seven officers, one RN petty officer, three DEMS ratings and twenty-two Indian seamen. Forty-three men, including Captian William McCracken and all his deck officers, were missing.

The lifeboat was overcrowded, it had lost its rudder, and its engine was out of action through being under water, so it was no more seaworthy than the two rafts. Ford, being the senior surviving officer, decided that, as the three craft were unable to help each other in any way, it would be best to split up, each then making the best possible progress to the east. It was agreed that whoever was picked up or reached land first would raise the alarm for the others. Within minutes of parting, they had lost sight of each other in the troughs of the swell.

Junior Fourth Engineer Douglas Goodall, unexpectedly finding himself elevated to command, albeit of a tiny wooden liferaft with a crew of two, resolved he would do his best. He was realist enough to accept that the *Larchbank* had gone down so quickly that there had been no time to send an SOS and that therefore no rescue ship was likely to come steaming over the horizon. The only route to safety lay eastwards, over 200 miles of rough seas to the coast of India. As the raft's only means of propulsion was by paddle, this was a formidible task. They would, however, be aided by the South-West Monsoon drift current, which at that time of the year, although very weak, was flowing due east. However, Goodall was an engineer, not a navigator, and was not aware of the current's existence. But what he lacked in knowledge, he made up for in determination.

When he came to examine the meagre resources at his disposal, Goodall's confidence received a severe shock. The underside of the raft had been damaged when it floated clear of the sinking ship, resulting in the puncturing of one of its fresh-water tanks, whose contents were polluted by sea water. The other tank had lost water by evaporation, or some other means, and contained no more than four pints. In the food tank, Goodall found one pound of biscuits, one tin of chocolate, two six-ounce tins of pemmican and one tin of malted milk tablets. With careful rationing, the food would last the three of them for many days, but the lack of drinking-water would be a critical factor in their survival. There was some small comfort to be found in the gear locker of the raft, which yielded a canvas weather screen and stanchions, three sleeping-bags, a torch, a tin of red distress flares, two measuring spoons and four graduated drinking-cups. After some deliberation, Goodall set the daily ration for each man at one ounce of water, three malted milk tablets, three pieces of chocolate, two biscuits and one spoonful of pemmican. He hoped this would ensure their survival for at least twenty days. If they had not reached land by then, they would escape through death.

It was not physically possible to paddle the raft continuously, so Goodall allocated specific hours during daylight for it. He had no way of knowing what progress they were making but, using the sun as a guide, endeavoured to keep the raft moving in an easterly direction. The days passed slowly and monotonously, with the small raft rising and falling uncomfortably on the interminable swell. Goodall kept an account of the passing of time by scratching a mark for each sunrise on one of the boards of the raft. On the fourth day it rained and, using the canvas screen, they collected half a gallon of water, thus doubling their chance of survival.

By 19 September, when they had been ten days adrift, it became apparent that Goodall's control of the rations had not been severe enough, for there remained only three pieces of chocolate, the pemmican, biscuits and malted milk tablets all having been consumed. Goodall then suggested to his companions that they attempt to catch fish, a number of which were swimming close to the raft. The Indians were apathetic, grumbling that they had neither fishing tackle nor bait. This did not deter Goodall. In his youth he had spent many a happy hour 'tickling' trout in the Scottish burns, patiently coaxing the speckled fish against the bank and into his hand. Lying face down on the raft – just as he had on the banks of a stream in his schooldays, he succeeded in trapping one of the small tropical fish against the side of the raft and, with a dexterity born of long practice, scooped it aboard. He quickly followed this with another. Using a scrap of the empty biscuit tin, he skinned the fish and cut them into small pieces. His companions, fearing they might be poisoned, at first refused to eat. When Goodall demonstrated that the raw fish was harmless, even palatable, they joined the feast with the enthusiasm of starving men at a laden table.

On the following day Goodall caught six more fish and found they were less salty if boned and dried in the sun. From then on, he provided daily meals for the three of them, but the water was again running short. To add to their troubles, a number of large sharks now began to follow the raft, perhaps sensing that the three men were growing weaker. As the days passed, the ugly predators – Goodall counted nine of them – grew bolder and frequently attacked the raft, attempting to overturn it. As they were crouched only a few inches above the water, this was a frightening experience for the survivors. At night the sharks changed their tactics, swimming close to the raft and slamming the water with their tails, so that the raft and its occupants were constantly lashed by spray. The obvious intent was to wear the survivors down by keeping them wet, miserable and sleepless. It was a ploy that might have worked had it not been for a defiant Goodall, who organized a defence of the raft, beating off the attackers with the weather-screen stanchions. But the sharks never gave up.

It rained again on the night of the 22nd, enabling the men to quench their raging thirst and collect sufficient water to last a few more days. Throughout, Goodall had kept the fresh-water ration at one ounce per man per day, which was barely enough to wet their parched throats, but just sufficient to sustain life. It was fortunate the weather was humid, for they perspired little and therefore preserved their bodily fluids.

A moment of ecstatic hope came on the morning of the 23rd. A ship was sighted but, although Goodall burned red distress flares, she sheered away and steamed off in another direction. The men on the heaving raft were near to tears with disappointment and frustration, but they did not give up hope. The sighting of the ship could mean they were at last in the shipping lanes and that others might follow in its wake.

For three long days and nights the ocean remained stubbornly empty. Only the persistent, cruising sharks kept company with the three emaciated, parched men who sprawled listlessly on their flimsy craft. Then, at sunset on the 26th, the roar of aircraft engines was heard, and a Sunderland flying-boat was seen flying low over the water. The survivors were roused from their stupor and galvanized into frantic action. They burned flares, waved and shouted until they were hoarse, but the giant plane flew past without deviation. As the raft was directly in the rays of the setting sun, Goodall concluded it was unlikely they had been spotted.

The night that followed was one of sheer misery for, although the weather had improved considerably, the number of sharks following the raft had increased to more than a dozen, nine of which were very large. During the dark hours, the assaults on the raft grew more frequent and frenzied. It was as though the predators sensed they were about to be cheated of their prey. Next morning it seemed the sharks' fears might be realized, for a ship appeared to the north. With his heart thumping, Goodall fumbled the last flare out of the tin, ignited it and held it high, while his two companions waved and shouted like madmen. They all cheered when the ship altered course towards them, and Goodall set off more flares, but their hopes were crushed when she sheered away again, ignoring their signals. The ship was soon hull-down on the southern horizon, zigzagging blissfully towards her destination.

Douglas Goodall, by now hardened to disappointment, was determined not to let despair get the better of him. For as long as he was able to catch fish – now the only food for the survivors – and for as long as the water held out, there was still hope. It was water that posed the greatest problem, for it had not rained for five days and they were down to little more than one pint between the three of them. As it was, five more days were to pass without rain or any further sign that help was at hand. When, on the afternoon of 2 October, another ship was sighted on the horizon to the north, heading towards the raft, Goodall was certain they must be directly in the path of ships using the Indian coastal shipping lanes. As there were no more flares left, he made a crude signal flag, using a paddle and a square of canvas. When the ship came near, he waved his flag vigorously and kept up the signalling for almost an hour, but again the ship sailed past, completely ignoring them.

The Indians had now reached the point where, through physical weakness, thirst and sheer heartbreak, they had lost all will to continue the struggle. But Goodall would not admit defeat. When the ship had gone out of sight, he balanced himself erect on the raft and quartered the horizon carefully. To his great relief, he saw another vessel coming in from the west, her bows pointed towards the raft. He goaded the others into taking up the paddles to keep the raft in the path of the approaching ship and took up his improvized flag again. After what seemed like a age, the ship, a large four-masted cargo vessel, was seen to alter towards them. She was soon abreast the raft, her crew lining the rails and cheering. A voice boomed out from the bridge, 'All right, lads! We will stop and pick you up.' These were the sweetest words Goodall had ever heard. With a triumphant shout, he hurled his signal flag at the still circling sharks and sat down on the raft, his mind at ease for the first time in twenty-three days.

The Danish motor vessel *Panama* launched a lifeboat, and half an hour later Goodall and the two Indian seamen were on board the ship being welcomed by her master, Captain Frederiksen. Their raging thirst was first slaked, then they were provided with hot baths, clothing and food in plenty. That night they slept the sleep of the exhausted between cool, clean sheets. Characteristically, Douglas Goodall's last thought before dropping off was that he would soon be able to return to sea in a ship of his own. The sudden loss of the *Larchbank* and the twenty-three days of hell he had endured had not broken his spirit.

As to the other *Larchbank* survivors, the six men on the larger raft had already been picked up by the British motor ship *Tahsinia* off Colombo on the morning of 27 September. Chief Engineer Ford and the twenty-three men in the disabled lifeboat had landed on the Indian coast on the night of the 28th. In all, thirty-three men survived the sinking of the *Larchbank*, but one of them, a Lascar seaman, died after arrival in Colombo.

Toshiaki Fukumura shifted his hunting-grounds to the Gulf of Aden for a while and there sank four ships. Six months later, on the afternoon of 12 February 1944, *1-27* was patrolling to the west of the Maldive Islands, when she sighted a small convoy.

Convoy KR 8, nearing the end of its 2500-mile passage from Mombasa to Colombo, was steaming in three columns of two. In the van, zigzagging wide on each bow, were the destroyers *Petard* and *Paladin*, who had joined that morning, while the ocean escort, the ageing cruiser HMS *Hawkins*, had dropped back to a less demanding role as lead ship of the port column. The Indian Ocean was on its best behaviour, sporting a light north-easterly breeze, blue skies and unlimited visibility; ideal for sunbathing but dangerously benign for a convoy of KR 8's calibre. The five merchant ships, under the direction of the Commodore in the 7513-ton *Khedive Ismail*, were all packed with troops. They were fat, sitting ducks, gliding across the oily swell at a vulnerable 13 knots.

Unaware of the scale of his good fortune, Fukumura began painstakingly to maneouvre *1-27* into position for an attack.

From the open bridge of HMS *Petard*, on the starboard bow of the convoy, the Officer of the Watch swept the horizon ahead with his binoculars, grimacing as the hot sun bore down on the back of his neck. Thoughts of tall, ice-frosted glasses on the terrace of Colombo's Galle Face Hotel were high in his mind when he turned aft to cast an eye over the convoy. This vision of self-indulgence was quickly wiped away as he caught sight of the periscope astern and to starboard of the lumbering merchant ships.

Petard's alarm gongs were already shattering the peace of the afternoon when two torpedoes slammed into the side of the *Khedive Ismail*, sending twin columns of dirty water and smoke soaring skywards. The trooper heeled drunkenly over to starboard and, within two minutes, had sunk, stern first.

With *Hawkins* giving cover, the remainder of the convoy scattered to the east, while *Petard* and *Paladin* raced in to attack with depth charges. They were too late, for without waiting to observe the result of his torpedoes, Fukumura had immediately dived deep. There followed a long cat-and-mouse game, with the two destroyers patiently stalking the enemy submarine, from time to time dashing in to drop patterns of depth charges, churning the once-placid ocean into an angry battlefield. But Fukumura was a wily foe, and, after about an hour, the escorts had lost all contact.

The Senior Officer of the escort, in HMS *Hawkins*, was by now becoming concerned for the safety of the other troopships and signalled *Paladin* to rejoin, leaving *Petard* to continue the search for the enemy. On her way back, *Paladin* lowered her boats near the wreckage-strewn area marking the end of the *Khedive Ismail* and proceeded to pick up survivors. There were precious few.

After carrying out a wide sweep to the westwards, which yielded no trace of the enemy, *Petard* returned to assist *Paladin* in the rescue work. While both ships were thus engaged, a large bubble of air welled to the surface close north-westwards of the wreckage. This might merely have been air escaping from the sunken ship; on the other hand, a submarine blowing her tanks would produce a similar effect.

Petard immediately broke away from the rescue operation and began sweeping with her Asdic in the vicinity of the bubble. No contact was made, but the destroyer persisted in her quest, searching in ever-widening circles. *Petard*'s commander was on the point of returning to the convoy when, with a great gush of air, *1-27* suddenly surfaced 1½ miles off the destroyer's starboard quarter.

By this time *Paladin* had recovered all survivors of the *Khedive Ismail* and was steaming to assist *Petard* in the search. With the submarine on the surface and apparently stopped, both escorts raced into the attack with all guns blazing. *Petard*, being closest to the enemy, made a run across her stern, hurling depth charges set to explode at fifty feet from her port thrower. These seemed to have no noticeable effect on the submarine.

1-27 was by now under way and some of her crew could be seen scrambling out of the conning tower, obviously intent on manning the deck gun. Fukumura did not intend to give up without a fight. But the heavy machine-guns of the attacking destroyers cut his men down before they even reached the casing.

It was then that the attack went seriously wrong for the British ships. While *Petard* moved away from the surfaced submarine in order to bring her big guns to bear, an over-enthusiastic *Paladin* closed in on the enemy at high speed, signalling she was going to ram. *Petard*'s commander, the senior officer on the spot, considered ramming to be too drastic and potentially dangerous an action at this point and signalled *Paladin* to hold back. His signal was received too late, and in attempting to abort the attack at the last minute, *Paladin* sheered away from *1-27*, put herself across the Japanese submarine's bow, and was herself rammed. She retired from the fray with her engine-room, steering gear and after-magazine flooded.

The fight now developed into a battle of wits between *1-27* and *Petard*. Although the submarine was plainly in serious trouble, for she was down by the stern and unable to man her 5-inch deck gun, she still had her bow and stern torpedo tubes. These worried *Petard*'s commander. For the next hour the two adversaries stalked each other, with *1-27* running in wide circles, striving to bring her torpedo tubes to bear on the destroyer. *Petard*, twisting and turning at high speed, fired some 300 rounds of 4-inch, smashing the submarine's deck gun and riddling her conning tower, but, being short of armour-piercing shells, she was unable to hole *1-27*'s pressure hull. The British commander considered closing the range to lob depth charges, but the threat of the enemy's torpedo tubes and the danger of repeating *Paladin*'s disastrous collision made him keep his distance.

Darkness was now coming on and, fearful that her quarry might escape with the setting sun, *Petard* was herself forced to resort to torpedoes. Even then the Japanese proved difficult to sink. Six of the destroyer's torpedoes missed, but the seventh found its mark and *1-27* blew up. When the tall column of water thrown up by the explosion subsided, the submarine had gone, leaving only a small patch of oil on the surface. A few minutes later there was a violent underwater explosion and more oil and some scraps of wreckage appeared.

Toshiaki Fukumura and his men had lost the three-hour-long battle but they had taken the honours. As they spiralled down to their last resting place they left behind them a scene of devastation and confusion. The *Khedive Ismail* was gone, taking almost 1500 men with her, the destroyer *Paladin* was crippled and in danger of sinking and the convoy had scattered. *1-27* would be remembered for a long time to come.

15   When Will We Learn?

We had experienced a full gale, and run the gauntlet of an attack by U-boats. And now we were homeward bound. It may have been a lack of visibility in the increasing darkness; it may have been merely foolish imagination. But as I walked along the deck towards the door of the engine-room I could have sworn I saw the shape of a ship. A British tramp she was, and her torn hull lay very low in the cross-seas. Her broken masts, her emptied lifeboat davits were ghostly mockeries of what they had been. And then a group of misted figures gathered from nowhere about her mainmast and hauled aloft a shadowy rag. I fancied I could hear that infinitely brave little group shout: 'The enemy had none of that colour!' And the tattered remnants of a Red Ensign fluttered in the night wind ...

As quick as it had come, the vision was gone. I had a feeling, out there in mid-ocean, that it was tragic the British Houses of Parliament could not send all those politicians, and the British industry all its experts and planners concerned with post-war policies, on one voyage in a salt-water tramp. Just one voyage, preferably between Britain and America, where they would see the real effects of an enemy torpedo on a ship carrying food and supplies; where they would see shattered seamen and shattered ships. Some of those ships should never have been afloat. But they were. And they went bravely on, voyage after eight-knot voyage, showing the Flag to an ever-decreasing number of astonished and awe-stricken crews of Hitler's U-boats.[1]

Those poignant words were written forty-four years ago by journalist and ship's engineer Warren Armstrong. World War II was then drawing to a close, a war which Great Britain had

191

entered with a vast fleet of over 4,000 merchant ships. When that bitter conflict ended and the final reckoning was made. 2,246 of those ships and 29,180 men had fallen to the enemy – twenty ships a week going down at the height of the Battle of the Atlantic. Britain had survived, but only through the supreme efforts of her merchant seamen, who had kept the sea lanes open at such great cost. Yet no one heeded the advice given by Warren Armstrong and so many others who had been in the thick of it. As the first peal of Victory bells rang out, politicians, planners and industrialists – not one having tasted life in a salt-water tramp – smartly turned their backs on Britain's Merchant Navy. All the sacrifices of those six punishing years, when Britain had been kept fed and armed for war, had been in vain. Those gallant, unsophisticated men, one in every three who had set sail from these shores, had died for nothing.

The danger was not immediately apparent, for, with a broken world to mend, the post-war years brought about a boom in shipping. Britain's merchant fleet prospered and grew fat again. By 1950, the Red Ensign flew over a quarter of the world's ships and looked set to regain its former eminence. The lot of the tramp-ship men improved dramatically. Most of the old ships had gone, sent to the bottom by the enemy's torpedoes. Their replacements would win no awards for excellence, but there was a mood of generosity in the air. This change of attitude came not through any sudden surge of gratitude on the part of the nation or her shipowners but as a direct result of the grievous losses suffered by the Merchant Navy during the war. The industry had lost a third of its trained workforce in the space of six years and was, in 1945, scraping the bottom of its manpower barrel. Accommodation became more spacious, and amenities were improved; many of the new-age tramps boasted the hitherto unheard-of luxury of fresh water piped to all cabins. Food, always an important part of a seaman's life, took a turn for the better. Curry and rice for breakfast and scouse for tea were out. Refrigeration had arrived and with it bacon and eggs, green salads and meat that needed no strong spices to disguise its rottenness. For the first time in history, British merchant seamen were guaranteed pay between voyages and awarded two days leave for every month on articles. After a brief tussle between unions and owners, the £10 a month extra the men had been paid in recognition of their willingness to run the gauntlet of the U-boats was added to their basic wage. From then on, wages and conditions of service went into an upward spiral in line with those ashore.

British merchant shipping peaked in 1975 at 50 million tons, and then, faced by competition it was not equipped to match, went into an unstoppable decline. As I write, the latest masthead count of Britain's merchant fleet stands at a mere 400 ships. The island nation which pioneered the carriage of goods by sea, and which once carried more than half the world's commercial trade in its bottoms, now occupies eleventh place in the international shipping league and is slipping lower day by day. Even tiny Cyprus and the backward People's Republic of China now have more ocean-going ships than Britannia. Two-thirds of Britain's exports and imports and one-third of her coastal trade have gone to foreign ships, possibly never to return. When the Falklands War came, Britain's Merchant Navy, for the first time in its long history, was found wanting. Committed at short notice to a retaliatory task force, the British government suffered the gross humiliation of having to charter foreign merchant tonnage to complete the 49-ship support fleet. In a recent NATO exercise in the North Sea, only one of the ten merchant ships in the British force flew the Red Ensign. The other nine were foreign ships chartered in by the Admiralty at a cost to the taxpayer of £6 million. At last, apathy has achieved what six years of war and the might of Hitler's U-boats failed to accomplish. Britain's Merchant Navy has become the skinny pariah of the seas, doomed to nibble at the fringes of world trade and incapable of sustaining her country in a time of need. How Warren Armstrong's ghosts of yesteryear must weep in their silent graves.

In the event of another war, the rundown of Britain's merchant fleet would have a catastrophic effect. The Soviet Union, the most likely aggressor, has a fighting navy of 2,000 surface ships and 400 submarines, plus a huge force of long-range bombers and missiles. Britain's Merchant Navy, already matched one for one by the submarines of the USSR, would last but a few short weeks. Nor can it be argued that the foreign ships now so eagerly mopping up the seaborne trade would come to Britain's aid. At the first bang of a hostile gun, 'these sceptred isles' would be declared off-limits and doomed to surrender or face starvation in splendid isolation.

There are those who say with confidence that war will never again come to Britain – and pray God they are right. Assuming their hypothesis is correct and the world lives in blessed peace for ever, it can be strongly argued that Britain no longer needs a merchant fleet of her own. It is now, in fact, cheaper to use foreign-flag ships, especially those under a flag of convenience, to move exports and imports. Why, then, should not the few remaining British shipowners turn shipbrokers and charter in foreign ships to carry their cargoes? On the face of it, this seems like sound economics. Foreign-owned ships, sailing under the convenience flags of Panama and Liberia, unfettered by irksome government restrictions and manned by cheap crews from the Far East, are able to operate at one-third the cost of a British ship; consequently their freight rates are lower. This must be to the advantage of the British economy.

And, again, the Soviet Union, whose merchant fleet has increased sixfold since 1960, would be only too willing to carry British goods at a very competitive price. Her ships are government-owned, heavily subsidized and impervious to losses. Already they have free access to British ports and are shifting cargoes at rates no Western shipowner can match.

Short-term, the gains might be attractive, but there would eventually be a price to pay. Cut-price ships often mean unskilled, poorly qualified and uninterested crews, poor maintenance and low safety standards. Proof of this can be seen in the annual casualty figures issued by the underwriters. Of the 200-plus ships lost every year – more than 1 million tons gross, those owned by the discount operators and manned by men from the Eastern Mediterranean, the Indian sub-continent and the Far East invariably head the list and account for over fifty per cent of the total. Maritime fraud is common in these ships; cargoes often 'disappear' on route, and ships founder in circumstances which can only be related to the amount of insurance they carry.

All Britain was shocked, and her remaining seafarers shamed, by the lapse in her traditional maritime excellence shown in the loss of the *Herald of Free Enterprise*. Lives were thrown away as a direct result of the infiltration of the cross-Channel ferries by the shore-conceived practice of passing the buck until it is conveniently mislaid. But that sad – and hopefully never-to-be-repeated – episode pales into insignificance alongside the recent sinking of the Philippines' ferry *Doña Paz*. More than 2,000 souls – and only God knows how many more – were lost when the *Doña Paz* went down off Manila after a collision resulting from apathy and incompetence. Both ships involved were manned by Filipino officers and ratings, the men who, in ever-increasing numbers, are now crewing the world's merchant ships, including 'flagged-out' British vessels.

The time is very near when the occupants of the British Isles must decide once and for all whether they still want, or in fact need, a Merchant Navy, for when the Red Ensign is lowered for good, there can be no going back. The only alternative will be foreign ships, foreign manned, and owned and operated by men whose standards are not British standards and whose loyalties lie far beyond Britain's shores. If the boom days return or war threatens, there can be no instant reincarnation of the British merchant fleet, for the expertise required to man the ships will no longer be there. Unskilled men might be shipped as ratings, but it takes many years to produce competent deck and engineer officers. Britain's remaining nautical schools are already empty of such men in training.

One is prompted to ask what has happened to that vociferous section of the British public which rushes to man the rhetorical barricades in the defence of so many less worthy causes. What of the mass of hysterical MPs who beat their breasts and shed tears of rage at any threat to their sacred-cow coal-mines and heavy industries? Ironically, the only shipping currently arousing public inerest in Britain is that of a bye-gone age. The rotting hulks of sailing-ships are being prised out of the mud by the score, to be lovingly restored and preserved at a cost which must make the wily shipping entrepreneurs of the Eastern Mediterranean fall about laughing.

When all the British merchantmen have gone – sold off at knock-down prices to maritime rivals, Britain may one day find herself looking down the wrong end of an extortionist's pistol. So long as ships are plentiful and cargoes short, freight rates will be competitive. When the wheel turns full circle – as it surely must, those foreign ships will set the rates and decide which countries they will serve. Britain, with no ships of her own, will then be at the mercy of the backstreet moguls of Piraeus and the stony-faced manipulators of the Kremlin. Her exports will become wholly uncompetitive and the price paid for imports prohibitive. Therein lies the road to a banana republic.

[1] See Armstrong, bibliography

Glossary

Nautical Terms

Abaft: Behind, in relation to something on the ship.
Abeam: At right angles to the fore and aft line of the ship.
Aft, After: Towards the stern.
After deck: That part of the maindeck abaft the bridge.
Airpipe: Pipe leading from ballast or fuel tanks to deck through which air escapes.
ASDIC: Submarine detection gear based on subsonic transmission.
Astern: Behind the ship.
Azimuth: Compass-bearing of sun, stars, etc.
Beam ends: When a vessel rolls very heavily to one side or the other she is said to be 'on her beam ends'.
Bilge: Channel at bottom of hold or engine-room into which sea water drains.
Binnacle: Stand in which ship's compass is set.
Black gang: Firemen and trimmers.
Block: Pulley through which wire or rope runs.
Boat deck: The deck on which lifeboats are stowed.
Boat stations: Stand by on boat deck to abandon ship.
Broach-to: To swing beam-on to wind and sea.
Bullk cargo: Loose homogeneous cargo e.g. sugar, grain, ores, etc.
Bulkhead: Steel or wooden partition between compartments.
Cargo liner: Ship employed on a regular and advertised trade.
Clipper stern: Cutaway stern reminiscent of the old clipper ships.
Coaming: Steel parapet around a hatchway.
Collision bulkhead: Steel watertight bulkhead nearest to the bows.
Corvette: Handy type of submarine hunter of about 900 tons. Much used by the Royal Navy for convoy escort duties.
Davit: Light crane at ship's side used for lowering or lifting lifeboat.
Deck service line: Pipe which carries sea water from engine-room to decks for fire-fighting or washing down.
DEMS: Defensively Equipped Merchant Ships. Initials used to

197

198

identify Royal Navy and Royal Artillery ratings seconded to merchant ships to man and maintain guns.

Derrick Crutch: Crutch-like support into which cargo derrick is lowered and secured when not in use.

Dog watch: The 4–8 p.m. watch is sometimes divided into two 'dog' watches. The first dog watch is 4–6 p.m., the second at 6–8 p.m.

Dunnage: Rough planks of wood used in stowing cargo.

Eight bells: Struck to signal the change of watches, i.e. at midnight, 4 a.m., 8 a.m., noon, 4 p.m., 8 p.m.

ETA: Estimated time of arrival.

Fall: Wire or rope purchase used for raising or lowering.

Flush deck: Deck running from bow to stern without interruption of forecastle or poop.

Focke-Wulf Condor: German four-engined reconnaisance bomber.

Forecastle: Crews' quarters at fore end of ship.

Forecastle head: Raised deck at fore end of ship.

Fore deck: That part of the main deck forward of the bridge.

Freeboard: Distance between water-line and main deck.

GRT: Gross registered tonnage.

Gunwale: The uppermost planking of an open boat.

Hatch beam: Portable steel beam supporting hatchboards.

Hatchboard: Heavy, steel-banded wooden board used to cover hatchway.

Hatchway: Opening in deck giving access to hold.

Heave-to: To stop the ship at sea.

HF/DF: High Frequency Direction Finder.

Jolly boat: Small general-purpose rowing-boat.

JU 88: German twin-engined bomber and torpedo-carrying aircraft.

Lascar: Indian seaman.

Lighter: Barge.

Light ship: Ship without cargo.

Main deck: The principal deck on a vessel having several decks.

Marlin spike: Pointed steel tool used to open the strands of a rope or wire when splicing.

Middle watch: Midnight to 4 a.m. and noon to 4 p.m.

MTB: Motor torpedo boat.

Painter: Lifeboat rope used to secure alongside or for towing.

Poop: Raised deck at after end of ship.

Scotch boiler: Smoke-tube boiler widely used in merchant ships.

Scupper: Drains at ship's side and in holds to carry off water.

Serang: Indian boatswain.

Sloop: Naval escort vessel, usually of about 1,000 tons.

Smoke float: Buoyant pyrotechnic giving off dense orange smoke. Standard equipment for ship's lifeboats and rafts.

Taffrail: Top of ship's rail, usually made of teak.

Thwart: Lifeboat seat.

Tiger bay: The Butetown district of Cardiff.

Tramp: A ship which is not engaged on a regular trade but carries cargo to any destination required.

Trim down: As in the case of a submarine, to fill ballast tanks in order to partly submerge the hull.

Tween deck: First deck below the main deck.

Well deck: Space on the main deck, either between the raised forecastle and the bridge or between the latter and the poop.

Whistle lanyard: Thin wire stretching from bridge to operating valve of ship's whistle.

Windlass: Steam or electric winch used for raising anchors.

Woodbine funnel: Tall, thin funnel peculiar to many tramp ships. The great height provided natural draught for the boiler furnaces.

W/T: Wireless telegraphy.

Merchant Navy Ranks (in order of seniority)

Captain/Master: In command.

Chief officer/First mate: Senior deck officer. Responsible for maintenance of hull and decks. Usually in charge of bridge on 4 to 8 watch.

Second officer/mate: Navigating officer. Keeps 12 to 4 watch.

Third officer/mate: Signals officer. Keeps 8 to 12 watch.

Apprentice: Deck officer in training and indentured to shipowner.

Radio officer: Operates and maintains wireless telegraphy equipment.

Chief engineer: Senior engine-room officer. Responsible to Captain for smooth running of engines and auxiliary machinery.

Second engineer: Responsible for maintenance of engines and auxiliary machinery. Usually keeps 4 to 8 watch in engine-room.

Third engineer: Keeps 12 to 4 watch and is also responsible for electrical repairs.

Fourth engineer: Keeps 8 to 12 watch in engine-room.

Fifth engineer: Usually on day work in engine-room and on deck, as required.

Chief steward: In charge of catering.

Boatswain: Senior rating on deck.

Carpenter: Responsible for all woodwork and plumbing above decks. Sounds ballast, fuel and freshwater tanks.

Quartermaster: Steers ship and keeps gangway watches in port.

Able seaman: Certified seaman.

Ordinary seaman: Uncertificated seaman.
Deck boy: Seaman in training.
Donkeyman: Senior engine-room rating.
Fireman: Attends boiler furnaces.
Trimmer: Supplies firemen with coal.
Greaser: Responsible for oiling and greasing engine.
Chief cook: In charge of galley.
Second cook: Assists chief cook and usually bakes bread.
Assistant steward: Cleans officers' cabins and serves in officers' saloon.

Bibliography

Armstrong, Warren, *Salt Water Tramp* (Jarrolds, 1945)
Bates, Lt. Cmdr L.M., *The Merchant Service* (Frederick Muller, 1945)
Bryant, Arthur, *The Turn of the Tide* (Collins, 1957)
Course, Captain A.G., *The Deep Sea Tramp* (Hollis & Carter, 1960)
Churchill, W.S., *The Second World War* (Cassel, 1948-52)
Cresswell, Captain John, *Sea Warfare 1939–45* (University of California Press, n.d.)
Hope, Stanton, *Ocean Odyssey* (Eyre & Spottiswoode, 1944)
Hurd, Sir Archibald, *Britain's Merchant Navy* (Odhams Press, 1943)
Mason, David, *U-Boat; the Secret Menace* (Macdonald, 1968)
Poolman, Kenneth, *Periscope Depth*, (Sphere Books, 1984)
Robertson, Terence, *The Golden Horseshoe*, (Evans Bros, 1955)
Rohwer, Jurgen, *Axis Submarine Successes 1939–1945* (Patrick Stephens, 1983)
Roskill, Captain S.W., *The War at Sea* (HMSO, 1954–61)
British Vessels Lost at Sea 1939–45 (HMSO, 1947)
The Battle of the Atlantic (HMSO, 1946)

Index